REVOLUTIONARY
DELAWARE

REVOLUTIONARY DELAWARE

Independence in the First State

Kim Rogers Burdick

THE
History
PRESS

Published by The History Press
Charleston, SC
www.historypress.net

Cover images: Front, *Delaware Committee of Safety Meeting Convened by Thomas Collins at Belmont Hall, in Smyrna, Delaware*. Painting by Walter J. Willoughby, circa 1925–30. *Photo by Gene Shaner, courtesy Delaware Division of Historical and Cultural Affairs*. Back, *The Delaware Blue Hens, Delaware Continental Regiment*, Paul Catts, artist. *Reproduced with permission of the Catts family. Photo by Christopher Mlynarczyk*.

First published 2016

ISBN 9781540201133

Library of Congress Control Number: 2016945829

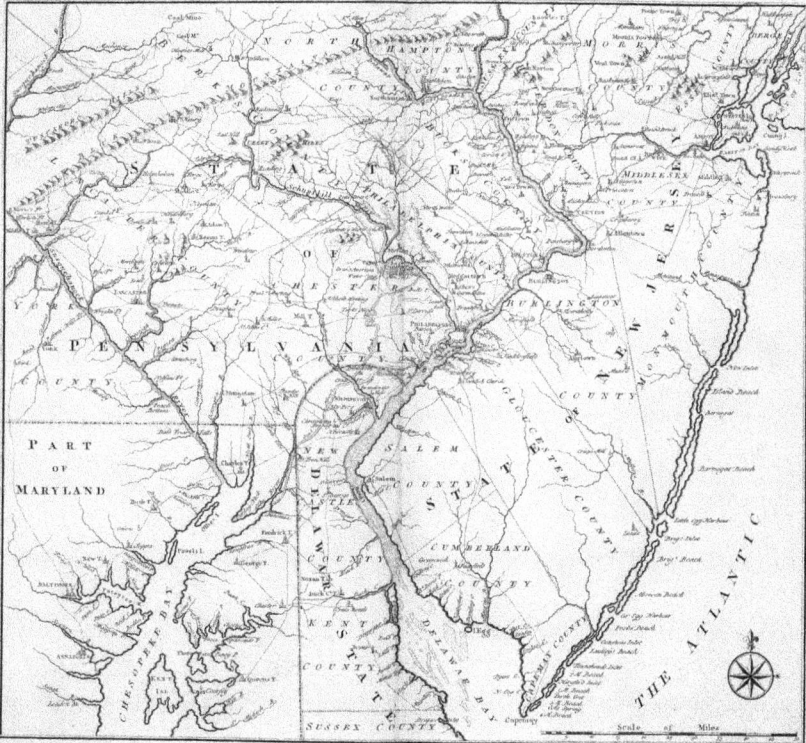

Detail of *A Chorographical Map*, circa 1778. H. Klockhoff, engraver, after Bernard Romans (circa 1720–circa 1784). *A Chorographical Map, of the Country, 'round Philadelphia Carte Particuliere, des Environs de Philadelphie.* Amsterdam, Chéz Covens et Mortier, et Covens, junior, 1778 [?]. *Society of Cincinnati.*

This book is dedicated to
Ralph and Teddy, Robert, Elizabeth, Martha and Punk.

CONTENTS

FOREWORD

Colonial Delaware was a fertile trading ground, sharing with Maryland and Virginia a peninsula hugged by the Chesapeake and Delaware Bays, the Delaware River and the Atlantic Ocean. At the geographic heart of Britain's thirteen American colonies, Delaware was, by 1764, positioned to play a critical role in the brewing rebellion.

During the war, Delaware hosted only one significant military engagement: the Battle of Cooch's Bridge. However, its people witnessed and participated in a torrent of action, and Delaware contributed one of the most important regiments to the Continental army; it fought throughout the middle and southern colonies in pivotal battles such as Trenton, Brandywine, Monmouth, Cowpens, Guilford Court House and Yorktown.

At the conclusion of the Revolutionary War, Delaware had a unique story to tell. By its location alone, the First State and its citizens arguably had the best vantage point from which to see the entire conflict. It was a true crossroads of news, private correspondence, confidential military matters, business, politics and travel. Delaware soldiers returned home from the front lines with an abundance of experiences to share.

For 250 years, many of Delaware's fascinating stories have been largely ignored in the shadows of epic battles and events dominating the pages of textbooks. Despite its rich and varied revolutionary history, Delaware barely gets a tip of the hat in most books about the Revolution. Fortunately, that isn't the case locally, where Delawareans have long shared great pride in their state's role in America's fight for independence. Schools are named for John Dickson, George Read and Thomas McKean. Lafayette's birthday is celebrated annually at the historic Hale Byrnes House near Stanton. Having visited Delaware and some of its revolutionary sites, I can personally vouch for the firm grip that locals have on their eighteenth-century history. It's as if they know Delaware is the best-kept secret of America's revolutionary heritage.

Historian Kim Burdick is letting the cat out of the bag. Unlike other, older books about Delaware's history, this is more than a compilation of Delaware soldiers' activities in far-away places. It's more than a history of Cooch's Bridge or Caesar Rodney's ride. It's a look at what happened on Delaware's homefront and a study of the broader impact of the American Revolution on Delaware's society and culture.

I've had the privilege of knowing Kim for nearly six years. She cares deeply about Delaware and works tirelessly to accurately understand and explain its role in the Revolution. Combining this love of local history with her scholarship in American folk culture, Kim has successfully advocated for revolutionary history told through the eyes of everyday people. With this book, she masterfully assembles a scholarly study of what happened in Delaware and to its people during the Revolution, bringing many critical views to light and telling us how ordinary people coped with extraordinary circumstances.

TODD ANDRLIK,
Editor in Chief, *Journal of American Revolution*,
www.allthingsliberty.com

ACKNOWLEDGEMENTS

If you can get enough Delawareans around a table, you can accomplish anything.
—*Delaware's unofficial state motto*

T his brief overview of what happened in Delaware during the twenty years of the Revolutionary War era is proof that the First State's venerable, but unofficial, motto is more truth than fiction. More than 150 pages, including photos and footnotes, is not enough space to tell this tale the way I would have liked, and 1 page is not enough to thank everyone who has helped and guided me through this long-term project.

My thanks begin with the directors, staffs and volunteers of the Delaware State Archives, Delaware Heritage Commission, the Delaware Historical Society, Morris Library at the University of Delaware, WILMAPCO, Friends Historical Library at Swarthmore College, 1st Delaware Regiment, Tillers International, the American Revolution Round Table of Northern Delaware, the David Library, W3R-US, the Lewes Historical Society, John Dickinson Plantation, Friends of Bombay Hook, Belmont Hall, Port Penn Area Historical Society, all the folks in historic New Castle, Historic Christiana, Pencader Heritage, Newark Historical Society, Quaker Hill, Brandywine Village, Claymont Stone School and, of course, the historic Hale Byrnes House.

I offer a special shout-out to Ralph and Teddy Burdick, Randy Goss, Don Hagist, Todd Andrlik, Hannah Cassilly, Chad Rhoad and Ryan Finn, as well as, in vaguely alphabetical order, David Ames, Bob Barnes, Kevin

ACKNOWLEDGEMENTS

Barni, Linda and Tracy Beck and Wes Jones, Julie Bell, Bobbi Britton, Riva Brown, Robin Brown, Carolyn Burlew, Angel Burns, Brian Cannon, Dick Carter, John Cartier, Wade Catts, Walt Chiquoine, Denise Clemmons, Ashley Cloud, Connie Cooper, Christopher Densmore, Mike DePaolo, Karen Dever, Joe DiBello, Donna and Milt Draper, Mary Anne Eves, Carl Fauser, Chuck Fithian, John Foskey, Michael Gallagher, Jack and Nancy Gardner, Guy Harrington, Denis Hehman, Gloria Henry, Ray Hester, Ann Horsey, Frank Ianni, Rachel Jirka, Ted Joslin, Jerry Kauffman, K. Lynn King, Joe Lake, Craig Lukezic, Bayard Marin, Debbie Martin, Chris Mlynarczyk, Susan Morikawa, Larry Nagengast, John Nagy, Nancy Parker, Karen Peterson, Willis Phelps, Jennifer Potts, Tyler Rudd Putman, Leigh Rifenburg, Lynn Riley, Brian Roberts, Martha Wooster Rogers, Carolyn Roland, Dick Roosenberg, Jeanne Sadot, Bob Selig, Gene Shaner, Diane Shaw, Cindy Snyder, Tom Sommers, Jim Thomen, Mary Torbey, Missy Vaughan, Jack Warren, Tom Welch, Barbara White, Marilyn Whittington, Kristen Wilczynski, Glenn Williams and Jim Yurasek.

There are many others who also deserve my deepest thanks, appreciation and admiration, and I salute all of you. As you know, I will be back to you with more requests and more questions about telling Delaware's story.

INTRODUCTION

Eighteenth-century Delaware was a prosperous place. Skiffs, sloops and schooners carrying grain, flour, passengers, merchandise and messages sailed daily up and down the Delaware River. Delaware-based trading vessels sailed freely back and forth to Philadelphia, the British Isles, Europe, Madeira and the West Indies. Local people sent raw materials to England for manufacture, traded with non-British entities and spent their profits on British-made goods. The Cape Henlopen lighthouse, paid for by a series of Philadelphia-based lotteries, was built of Brandywine granite shipped down from Wilmington. It was a fine investment.

Delaware's history and economy were part of a larger matrix. In the eighteenth century, New Castle, Kent and Sussex Counties were officially known as the Lower Three Counties of Pennsylvania, and many residents had homes on both sides of today's borders. The "Penman of the American Revolution, John Dickinson of Pennsylvania," was Delaware's John Dickinson. When war broke out, Dickinson held the rank of brigadier general in the Pennsylvania Militia. Temporarily ostracized for refusing to sign the Declaration of Independence, he returned home to Delaware and served with the Delaware Militia during the Battle of Brandywine. Dickinson would later serve both as governor of Delaware and as governor of Pennsylvania. Similarly, Thomas McKean served in Delaware's first House of Assembly, as president of Delaware, as president of the Continental Congress and later as governor of Pennsylvania.

Bear Swamp, Bombay Hook. *Karen Sinar Dever.*

Originally settled by the Dutch and Swedes, and later controlled by William Penn's family, Delaware, in the eighteenth century, had a large percentage of inhabitants who were Quakers and Anglicans and had no significant objections to the way they had been ruled by the British government. As a proprietary colony stretching 110 miles south from Philadelphia along the west bank of the Delaware River and Bay, what happened in Pennsylvania, New Jersey, Maryland, Virginia and Massachusetts, as well as the other colonies, was important to Delaware.

From 1682 to 1776, Delaware was officially known as Three Lower Counties of Pennsylvania. In 1776, these three counties declared independence both from England and from Pennsylvania, shrugging off the long-term control of the Penn family. When Britain reversed its longstanding policy of benign neglect, fear and anger caused by uncertainty, by the lurking presence of British warships and naval battles in the Delaware River and Bay and by the competing needs of civilians and soldiers for food, clothing, shelter and supplies made the American Revolution a traumatic time. Many Delawareans clung to the past and wished that the war would go away. The

Revolutionary era was long, and it would take years for the small state to regain its sense of balance.

Children born in the year of the Stamp Act were twelve years old when the Declaration of Independence was signed. Many of these children— as well as their big brothers, fathers, grandfathers, cousins and uncles— enlisted in the Continental army or joined local militias, celebrating their twentieth birthdays by marching home from war.[1] Some grew up as refugees fleeing with their families to Canada or England. Others lived in families quietly waiting out the war, moving or taking cover as needed in Delaware's swamps and marshes.

John Adams famously said, "I should say that full one third was averse to the revolution; An opposite third gave themselves up to an enthusiastic gratitude to France. The middle third, always averse to war, were rather lukewarm both to England and France." This was apparently written about the French Revolution, not our own,[2] but Adams's "rule of thirds" was equally applicable to Delawareans' attitudes toward the American Revolution.

Chapter 1

REINING IN THE COLONIES

The Stamp Act and Other Measures

In 1764, in Britain's attempt to pay off debts incurred during the French and Indian War, more than 150 years of benign neglect came abruptly to an end as the cash-strapped British Parliament unexpectedly began taxing the American colonies. The British point of view is not difficult to grasp—the taxes being levied were lower than those asked of mainland English citizens, and the revenue raised from taxing the colonies would be used to pay for America's defense and would barely cover one-third the cost of maintaining British troops stationed in the colonies. The colonists, however, questioned the need for these troops. The French and Indian War was over, and they wondered why they should pay Britain's debts for a war most had not asked for or wanted. Parliament's attempts at revenue generation caused ripples of doubt and concern.[3] Residents of the Lower Three Counties of Pennsylvania were among the first to complain.

George Read of New Castle, Delaware, was a member of what became known as the Court Party. This largely Anglican sector worked well with the colonial proprietary government and favored reconciliation with the British government. In 1764, Read wrote to a colleague in London:

> *The stamp-act you made on your side of the water hath raised such a ferment among us—that is, among one and all of the Colonies on the continent—that I know not when it will subside. Before you will receive this I doubt not but you will see in our public papers the opposition generally made to the distribution of the stamp-papers, and to these*

British political cartoon, 1777. "Poor old England endeavoring to reclaim his wicked American children." *British Cartoon Prints Collection, Library of Congress.*

publications I shall refer to you for particulars.... This will naturally lead them into measures to live as independently as possible, [and] they will, gradually, go into the making of woolens and ironmongery, your two great branches of manufactory.... The spirit has seized them already and prevails surprisingly. Homespun cloth is worn as well by the beaux as the men of gravity of all ranks, and though only fashion with the first, it will soon grow into habit, which, once fixed, will not be readily changed. From this consideration alone every friend to the mother country and the Colonies ought to wish and to afford a helping hand to obtain an alteration in the late system of politics in England.[4]

Word quickly spread among ordinary folks that trouble was brewing. In Lewes, Delaware, protestors calling themselves the "Sons of Liberty" met in March 1766. Demanding the keys to the Sussex County Courthouse, they took possession of the county's magazine, its drum and its colors. They fired cannons, raised huzzahs and drank toasts to King George. They asserted their loyalty to the king in resolutions but insisted that the British government did not have the right to tax the colonies without their consent. Like their counterparts in New England, Sussex Countians claimed that the Stamp

Act was "unconstitutional, destructive of our natural rights and liberties, and introductive of base servitude to the latest posterity."[5]

Largely in reaction to earlier protests by British businessmen, the Stamp Act was repealed on March 18, 1766. Thomas McKean, George Read and Caesar Rodney wrote to King George III, expressing Delaware's gratitude for this event and assuring him of the Lower Three Counties' loyalty to the Crown. Jubilation, however, was premature.

Britain rescinded the Stamp Act but enacted a substitute measure. The new "Declaratory Act" was tailored specifically to make it clear that parliamentary law took precedence over colonial charters and would serve as a reminder to the colonies that they had no say in the matter: "That all resolutions, votes, orders, and proceedings, in any of the said Colonies or plantations, whereby the power and authority of the parliament of Great Britain, to make laws and statutes as aforesaid, is denied, or drawn into question, are, and are hereby declared to be, utterly null and void to all intents and purposes whatsoever."[6]

American colonists were now forbidden to produce their own iron or use a ship, boat, carriage or packhorse to carry wool, or any product of which

Political cartoon, circa 1766, showing a funeral procession on the banks of the Thames, with warehouses in the background. George Grenville carries a coffin inscribed, "Miss Ame-stamp. Born 1765 died 1766." *British Cartoon Prints Collection, Library of Congress.*

wool formed a part, across the line of one province to another or bring wool across a river. Anger grew and spread throughout Delaware as the inherent unfairness of Britain's new policies and the impact this would have on the local economy became more and more apparent. Thomas McKean, George Read and Caesar Rodney wrote again to King George III, protesting the Declaratory Act.

Chapter 2

THE LIBERTY SONG

I n 1767–68, John Dickinson's "Letters from a Farmer in Pennsylvania to the Inhabitants of the British Colonies" began to appear in Philadelphia's newspaper, the *Pennsylvania Chronicle*. The first significant call for colonial unity in the face of British oppression, Dickinson's series of fourteen letters pointed out the economic folly of revenue laws that ignored the rights of Englishmen living in the colonies. He noted that these acts ignored the British constitution, and he predicted future conflict between the colonies and the mother country. These letters were sold in pamphlet form in Philadelphia, Boston, New York and even in London, with a brief preface written by Benjamin Franklin. Other printings followed in Paris and Dublin.

Dickinson also wrote a rousing, catchy drinking/protest song to the tune of the popular British naval anthem, "Heart of Oak":

"THE LIBERTY SONG"
John Dickinson, 1768

Come join hand in hand brave Americans all
and rouse your bold hearts at fair Liberty's call;
No tyrannous acts shall suppress your just claim,
Or stain with dishonour America's name.
In Freedom we're born and in Freedom we'll live,
Our purses are ready,
Steady, Friends, Steady.

THE PATRIOTIC AMERICAN FARMER.

J-N D-K-NS—N Esq.ᵣ BARRISTER at LAW:

Who with Attic Eloquence and Roman Spirit hath Aserted, The Liberties of the BRITISH Colonies in America.

Tis nobly done, to Stem Taxations Rage,
And raise, the thoughts of a degen'rate Age,
For Happiness, and Joy, from Freedom Spring,
But Life in Bondage, is a worthless Thing.

Printed for & Sold by R. Bell. Bookseller

John Dickinson (1732–1808). *Special thanks to John Dickinson Plantation, Dover, Delaware.*

Not as slaves, but as Freemen our money we'll give.
Our worthy Forefathers—Let's give them a cheer
To climates unknown did courageously steer;
Thro' Oceans, to deserts, for freedom they came,
And dying bequeath'd us their freedom and Fame.
Their generous bosoms all dangers despis'd,
So highly, so wisely, their Birthrights they priz'd;
We'll keep what they gave, we will piously keep,
Nor frustrate their toils on the land and the deep.
The Tree their own hands had to Liberty rear'd;
They liv'd to behold growing strong and rever'd;
With transport they cry'd; "Now our wishes we gain
For our children shall gather the fruits of our pain."

This bumper I crown for our Sovereign's health
And this for Britannia's glory and wealth;
That wealth and that glory immortal may be,
If she is but just—and if we are but free.

Come join hand in hand brave Americans all,
And rouse your bold hearts at fair Liberty's call;
No tyrannous acts shall suppress your just claim,
Or stain with dishonour America's name.

In Freedom we're born and in Freedom we'll live,
Steady, Friends, Steady.
Our purses are ready,
Steady, Friends, Steady.[7]

On August 17, 1769, New Castle County residents met at Christiana Bridge, where they signed an agreement stating they would not sell English goods or trade with any who did. The document was signed by "Order, and in Behalf of the Grand Jury for the County, in August Sessions, 1769, by SAMUEL PATTERSON, Foreman." Perhaps the most chilling part of their decision was the following clause: "That any one of us, who shall willfully break this Compact, shall have his name published in the public News Papers, as a Betrayer of the civil and religious Rights of Americans, and be forever after deemed infamous, and an Enemy to his Country."[8]

Being an enemy to "this country" was a new concept. England had been "our country" for many years, but the country being spoken of was not England. This broadside was referring to thirteen separate colonies that had never thought of themselves as a "country," and the enemies referred to were friends, neighbors and relatives who believed that they were doing the right thing by remaining loyal to the king. The ominous phrase would be repeated throughout the war.

The killing of five Bostonians by British regulars on March 5, 1770, was the culmination of tensions building since royal troops had first appeared in Massachusetts to enforce the Townshend Acts. Known as the Boston Massacre, this event became the springboard for united colonial rebellion. A few weeks later, in April 1770, the British government tried a clever tactic: reducing the cost of government-owned East India Company tea so that even after the tax, this was the lowest price available. This, Britain thought, would induce colonists to buy the tea, inadvertently accepting Parliament's right to tax them. The colonies stubbornly clung to their boycotts. Protests continued.

No More Tea

The last straw came in September 1773 when news came that East India Company tea shipments were on their way to America. Measures were taken in the colonial ports to prevent the landing and sale of the tea. A Philadelphia-based decree stated that

> *the resolution lately entered into by the East India Company, to send out their tea to America subject to the payment of duties on its being landed here, is an open attempt to enforce the ministerial plan, and a violent attack upon the liberties of America...Resolved—that whoever shall, directly or indirectly, countenance this attempt, or in any wise aid and abet in unloading, receiving, or vending the tea sent, or to be sent, out by the East India Company while it remains subject to a duty here, is an enemy to his country.*[9]

When word came that a British tea ship, the *Polly*, was on its way from England to Philadelphia, it was obvious that the first Americans to have contact with it would be Cape Henlopen's river pilots. Their job was to lead oceangoing vessels through the treacherously shoal-ridden Delaware River and Bay. Captain Ayres of the *Polly* and the river pilots were warned in print, under threat of being tarred and feathered, not to bring the tea ship upriver to Philadelphia. A handbill read, in part:

> *You are sent out on a diabolical Service; and if you are so foolish and obstinate as to complete your Voyage, by bringing your Ship to Anchor in this Port, you may run such a Gauntlet as will induce you, in your last Moments, most heartily to curse those who have made you the Dupe of their Avarice and Ambition.*
>
> *What think you, Captain, of a Halter around your Neck—ten Gallons of liquid Tar decanted on your Pate—with the Feathers of a dozen wild Geese laid over that to enliven your Appearance? Only think seriously of this—and fly to the Place from whence you came—fly without Hesitation—without the Formality of a Protest—and above all, Captain Ayres, let us advise you to fly without the wild Geese Feathers.*

On December 25, Captain Ayres was intercepted and brought into Philadelphia. Two days later, a large crowd assembled on the statehouse lawn. Nearly seven hundred chests of tea that had been ordered by the Philadelphia Quaker firm of James & Drinker were formally refused, and Ayres was escorted back to his ship at the Arch Street Wharf. Within two hours, the *Polly* was loaded with fresh provisions and water and sent away to "convey the tea back to its old rotting-place in Leadenhall Street."

The Philadelphia Tea Party was relatively nonviolent and no tea was destroyed, but when on March 28, 1774, Parliament closed the Port of Boston in retribution for the more dramatic Boston Tea Party, fear reverberated across the greater Delaware Valley. If Britain could shut down the Port of Boston, it could shut down any Philadelphia port or any other colony's port.

Parliament, in an effort to prevent unified colonial resistance by isolating Boston, imposed even more laws. This third set of British laws, known as the Coercive Acts, restricted Massachusetts's rights to its traditional town meetings, revoked its colonial charter and blockaded Boston's port. Parliament's newest goal was to restore order in Massachusetts and punish Bostonians for dumping nearly $1 million worth of tea (in today's money) into Boston Harbor. Included in these sanctions was the Administration of Justice Act, which made British officials immune to criminal prosecution in Massachusetts, and the Quartering Act, which required colonists to house and quarter British troops on demand, including in their private homes.

British political cartoon, 1777. "Old Maid Drinking Tea." *British Cartoon Prints Collection, Library of Congress.*

The Coercive Acts backfired. The other colonies anxiously monitored the events in Boston, finding it difficult to argue that the Crown was not interested in stripping away American civil liberties. American sentiment shifted further and further away from Parliament. The Committees of Correspondence were buzzing. People all over the colonies protested, collecting money and supplies for Boston and forming "Congresses" to mobilize resistance to the Crown. It was reasonable to fear that Britain would close area ports. Philadelphia's massive commercial activity moved more than 88,000 tons through the Port of Philadelphia, and in 1772, British statistics recorded forty-four topsail ships and forty-six sloops bringing in 4,363 tons of goods to New Castle. Residents of all ranks and faiths in the Lower Three Counties intuitively understood the economic and political damage that England had done by closing the Port of Boston.

Yankee Doodle Went to Town a-Riding on a Pony

Meetings of freeholders and inhabitants were conducted in Delaware that summer. Thirteen men who had been, or were then, assemblymen were chosen in each of the Three Counties to serve as members of a Committee of Correspondence.[10] In June, Thomas McKean of New Castle organized the first mass meeting to discuss Britain's treatment of Boston. More than five hundred people attended. The New Castle group drew up a seven-point program that was forwarded to Kent and Sussex Counties for their input and read, in part:

> *1774. June 29. Meeting of Freeholders and Inhabitants of New Castle County. Thomas McKean, Chairman.*
>
> *1. Resolved, That the act of Parliament for shutting up the port of Boston is unconstitutional, oppressive to the inhabitants of that town, dangerous to the liberties of the British Colonies, and that we consider our brethren at Boston as suffering in the common cause of America.*
> *2. That a Congress of deputies from the several Colonies in North America is the most probable and proper mode of procuring relief for our suffering brethren, obtaining redress of American grievances, securing our rights and liberties, and re-establishing peace and harmony between Great Britain and these Colonies on a constitutional foundation.*
> *3. That a respectable committee be immediately appointed for the county of New Castle, to correspond with the sister Colonies, and with the other counties in this government, in order that all may unite in promoting, and endeavoring to obtain, the great and valuable ends mentioned in the foregoing resolution.*

New Castle Court House. *Jim Yurasek, Delaware Division of Historical and Cultural Affairs.*

> *4. That the committee, now to be chosen, consist of thirteen persons, to wit: Thomas McKean, John Evans, John McKinley, James Latimer, George Read, Alexander Porter, Samuel Patterson, Nicholas Van Dyke, Thomas Cooch, Job Harvey, George Monroe, Samuel Platt, and Richard Cantwell, and that any seven of them may act.*
>
> *5. That the said committee immediately set on foot a subscription for the relief of such poor inhabitants of the town of Boston as may be deprived of the means of subsistence by the act of Parliament, commonly styled the Boston Port-Bill. The money arising from such subscription to be laid out as the committee shall think will best answer the end proposed.*[11]

On July 6, 1774, a second large meeting was held at the New Castle Courthouse. Thomas McKean was chosen as chairman, and a committee was appointed to meet with "the sister Colonies…in order that all may unite in promoting and endeavoring to attain the rights of the Colonies as British subjects."[12] The committee was to direct the delegates to meet in New Castle no later than August 1. In response, the Kent County delegates wrote to their Sussex counterparts:

We are sensible of the unreasonableness and impropriety of the conduct of the New Castle people on this occasion, in undertaking to dictate to you and us a mode of conduct and also fixing a place for our meeting, without our consent very convenient for themselves but very inconvenient for us: we think they might have been more polite.[13]

On July 23, 1774, a meeting of freeholders and other inhabitants of Sussex County met at the courthouse in Lewes. McKean, aware of their irritation, deliberately attended the meeting, where he spoke at length, passionately listing the rights of colonists under some twenty-seven headings and pointing out the governmental measures that Britain had violated. He noted the curbs on the Three Lower Counties on Delaware's iron industry and made a particular point of the fact that farmers were prohibited from carrying their own wool across a ferry, "though the rivers, waters, havens, etc. are given to us by our Charters," emphasizing the impact on the hat and wool trades. His talk produced the desired effect, with Sussex County agreeing to go along with the other two counties.[14]

In response to a formal invitation by Kent Countian Speaker Caesar Rodney, the members of the Delaware Assembly agreed to meet in New Castle on August 1, 1774. Their collective resolutions condemned the British Parliament for restricting manufactures in the colonies, for taking away property from the colonists without their consent, for introducing the arbitrary powers of the excise into the customs in America, for making all revenue causes triable without a jury and under a single dependent judge and for passing the Coercive Acts. The convention named Caesar Rodney, Thomas McKean and George Read, "or any two of them," as delegates from the Lower Three Counties to the Congress that was to be held at Philadelphia on the first Monday of September 1774. John Dickinson, who had been elected to the Pennsylvania Assembly in 1762, would serve as a Pennsylvania delegate.

The First Continental Congress met in Carpenter's Hall in Philadelphia for eight weeks, from September 5 to October 26, 1774. Previously, the American colonies had acted as independent entities and had not previously worked together as a team, but every colony except Georgia sent delegates. The First Continental Congress represented a broader cross section of colonial opinion than its successors. Delegates had been elected by the people, by the colonial legislatures or by their committees of correspondence. Among others who attended were John and Samuel Adams of Massachusetts and George Washington, Patrick Henry and Richard Henry Lee of Virginia.

Washington, on his way to the meeting, noted in his diary on September 3, 1774, "Dined at Buck Tavern (Carson's) and lodged at New Castle."

The first few weeks were spent in discussion and debate. As delegates wrapped up their second week in Philadelphia, a rider blew into town. It was Paul Revere, delivering a copy of a declaration issued a few days before by the leaders of Suffolk County, Massachusetts. The Suffolk Resolves, drafted by Joseph Warren, denounced the Coercive Acts of Parliament, called for formation of militia units and demanded an embargo on trade with Britain. These resolves set the tone for the next month of joint deliberations:

Whereas the power but not the justice, the vengeance but not the wisdom, of Great Britain, which of old persecuted, scourged and exiled our fugitive parents from their native shores, now pursues us, their guiltless children, with unrelenting severity; and whereas, this then savage and uncultivated desert was purchased by the toil and treasure, or acquired by the valor and blood, of those our venerable progenitors, who bequeathed to us the dear-bought inheritance, who consigned it to our care and protection—the most sacred obligations are upon us to transmit the glorious purchase, unfettered by power, unclogged with shackles, to our innocent and beloved offspring.[15]

Mary Vining (1756–1821), 1775.
Delaware Public Archives.

The First Continental Congress reminded all colonists to avoid using British goods and asked each colony to establish Committees of Inspection to enforce the boycott. It adjourned on October 26, 1774, ten years after the Stamp Act had been initiated.

Delaware's Country Party was largely Ulster-Scot, centered in New Castle County, and quickly advocated independence from the British. In spite of being members of the Anglican, Kent County gentry, Rodney and his brother, Thomas Rodney, increasingly aligned themselves with the Country Party, a distinct minority in Kent County. As such, Caesar Rodney generally worked in partnership with Thomas McKean from New Castle County and sometimes in opposition to Court Party supporter George Read. Caesar Rodney influenced his cousin Mary Vining, known as the "Belle of Delaware," to support the revolt from England, and she frequently served as hostess for Rodney's meetings and receptions. Legend has it that in this capacity, she met and fell in love with Revolutionary War hero Anthony Wayne.

On January 26, 1775, another provincial convention was held in Philadelphia. This one was designed to push for enforcement of the measures recommended by Congress and to advocate for the promotion of American manufactures, especially of gunpowder. In Delaware, the community pulled together to send relief money to Boston.

George Read of New Castle wrote to a contact in Boston:

> *1775, Feb 5. I am to inform you that Nicholas Van Dyke and myself were appointed to receive the donations of the people of the county for the relief of the poor of Boston, and that we now have in our hands upward of nine hundred dollars, which we have endeavored to remit to you by way of bills to be drawn by mercantile persons in Philadelphia, who transact business with your colonists, and were safe hands; but upon a strict inquiry we can find none amongst them willing to draw any bills for some time to come, lest they should distress their correspondents by drafts too early for the season of business. Upon this disappointment we had thoughts of purchasing English bills, but upon reflection doubted whether you might not be losers by the exchange; therefore, I must request the advice and direction of your committees as to the most speedy and acceptable mode of remittance... You may be assured that it is from a people who sincerely sympathize with you in your distresses, and are anxious for your relief. Please to present my compliments to Messrs. Cushing, Adamses, and Pain [sic], and I am, with esteem,*
>
> *Your most obedient and humble servant, George Read*

Although many local people contributed to the Boston Relief Fund, in Delaware daily life went on at its usual pace. On April 1, Joseph Tatlow and Thomas Henderson optimistically announced that they had "established a stage line for the term of seven years to carry on business between Philadelphia and Baltimore, via New Castle and Frenchtown."[16]

Parliament extended the Boston Port Act to all of Massachusetts and insisted that New England's trade was to be limited to Britain and the British West Indies. Trade with other nations was to be prohibited effective July

1, 1775, and New England ships barred from the North Atlantic fisheries effective on July 20. A new Port Act was also passed, deliberately affecting New Jersey, Virginia, Maryland and South Carolina, all known by the British to be rebellious states. Congress now began a protracted debate on whether all British customhouses should be closed. Although the Three Lower Counties of Pennsylvania were not specifically mentioned in the British missive, Thomas McKean was emphatic that Delaware and other exempted colonies should close their ports and boycott British goods:

> *I have four reasons for putting the favoured Colonies upon a footing with the rest. The 1ˢᵗ, is to disappoint the Ministry. Their design was insidious. 2. I would not have it believed by Ministry or other Colonies that those Colonies had less virtue than others.*
>
> *3. I have a reconciliation in view, it would be in the power of those Colonies; it might become their interest to prolong the war.*
>
> *4. I believe Parliament has done or will do it for us, i.e. put us on the same footing. I would choose that the exempted Colonies should have the honor of it. Not clear that this is the best way of putting them upon a footing. If we should be successful in Canada, I would be for opening our trade to some places in G.B., Jamaica, etc.*[17]

Raising the Liberty Pole. Painted by F.A. Chapman, 1776, engraved by John C. McRae, New York. *Library of Congress.*

When news was received in London that colonies outside New England had formed a Continental Association, a forty-four-gun British frigate began patrolling, interrupting commerce, collecting intelligence and chasing smugglers. An express rider arrived in Philadelphia with news that at Lexington and Concord, not far from Boston, British regulars had fought American minutemen on April 19. The Provincial Congress in Massachusetts requested that additional American soldiers be mobilized.

The Second Continental Congress was called to order on May 10, 1775, with George Read, Caesar Rodney and Thomas McKean representing the Lower Three Counties of Pennsylvania and John Dickinson serving as a Pennsylvania delegate. Congress placed the colonies in a state of defense, and on June 15, the representatives of the American colonies unanimously voted to appoint George Washington general and commander in chief of a Continental army. Militia companies were formed and exercised in all the open parks and squares, the manufacture of gunpowder and cannons was urged forward and preparations were made to obstruct navigation of the Delaware River.

Chapter 3

THE RIGHT AND PROPER THING TO DO?

With a British warship patrolling the Delaware River and Bay, the stability of life in the Lower Three Counties—the things that had always been "the right and proper thing to do"—was being criticized seemingly without reason. Ordinary law-abiding people—mothers, fathers, farmers, housewives, shop keepers, craftsmen, laundresses and others, as well as merchants and society people—were frightened by the news from Philadelphia. Terrified that the Continental Congress had gone too far, most clung to their religious faiths and prayed that the radicals would not overstep.

Most of Delaware's long-term residents were Quakers and Anglicans. Now the burgeoning Scotch-Irish Presbyterian population was beginning to push them out of the way. The developing religious schism was noted even in Britain. British Whig Horace Walpole quipped to a friend, "Cousin America has run off with a Presbyterian minister," and Ambrose Serle, civilian secretary to Admiral Lord Richard Howe, agreed, saying, "Republican Presbyterianism can never heartily coalesce with Monarchy and Episcopacy. Dissenting preachers, fire-breathing to a man, inculcate war, bloodshed and massacre."

Anglican missionaries, newly arrived in the Lower Three Counties, emphasized the need to combat America's growing numbers of contentious Presbyterians. One layman noted that "they make Presbyterian Ministers with as much ease as a Countrywoman sets eggs under Hen and Hatches Chickens." The Presbyterians, citing the Anglicans' opposition to the repeal

Left: King George III (1738–1820). William Pether, engraver, and Thomas Frye, artist, 1762. *Library of Congress.*

Below: Interior, Old Christ Church (Old Lightwood), built in 1722 and located at the edge of Chipman's Pond, Laurel, Delaware. *Delaware Public Archives.*

of the Stamp Act, argued, "We dare not yet trust Bishops with our Liberties," and both Anglicans and Presbyterians mistrusted the pacifist Quakers.

Pennsylvania had been deliberately established as a safe harbor for Quakers. As the squabbles over British regulations increased, they tried to stay neutral. Even in Philadelphia, where the Society of Friends had been prominent for nearly one hundred years, Quakers who combined political power with spiritual leadership were now the exception rather than the rule. As discontent grew, it became harder to stay within the confines of pacifism. William Penn's words must have been quoted often: "Right is right, even if everyone is against it, and wrong is wrong, even if everyone is for it."

In later years, Thomas McKean wrote to his colleague, John Adams, that Delaware's Patriot movement had developed as a way to contest a corrupt political system that gave Quakers unrepresentative political power. He further claimed that Loyalism in the First State arose from Anglican missionaries who had explained the rebellion as "a plan of Presbyterians to get their religion established."[18]

Life in the Lower Three Counties became increasingly uncertain when even the monetary system began to change. Caesar Rodney wrote to his younger brother, Thomas, on June 20, "I can now let you into a part of our proceedings in Congress—We have ordered two millions of dollars to be struck as Continental paper currency, for the defraying the expenses of defending our Constitutional Rights and privileges."[19]

Among those hardest hit was forty-five-year-old Thomas Robinson of Sussex County, who as a member of Delaware's Committee of Correspondence in October 1773 had protested the Boston Port Bill. Robinson was a well-respected citizen. A store owner who owned more than one thousand acres of land in Indian River and Rehoboth Hundreds, he was a locally elected member of the Delaware Assembly. When Sussex County formed its Committee of Correspondence, witnesses testified that Robinson had called the Continental Congress "an unconstitutional body of men." The fact that he was correct, and that the governing constitution of that era was the British constitution, was outside the scope of discussion. Suddenly it was resolved that Thomas Robinson was "an enemy to his country." Local authorities demanded that all persons break away from commercial relations with him.[20] It would seem that some unrelated personal grudges had also been brought to the table.

What Robinson had called the "unconstitutional body of men" was actually writing a letter of peace and reconciliation to the king of England. The Olive Branch Petition—drafted in Philadelphia by Benjamin Franklin,

Thomas Jefferson, John Rutledge, John Jay, and William Livingston—was first presented to the committee of Congress on June 24, 1775, but was not approved. Thomas Jefferson rewrote the document in simpler words, and John Dickinson edited and refined it.

In July 1775, the carefully worded memorial and protest was forwarded to London. The Olive Branch Petition reasserted American loyalty to the Crown and appealed directly to King George III "with all humility submitting to your Majesty's wise consideration," hoping for "a happy and permanent reconciliation," and it also asked that "in the meantime…such statutes as more immediately distress any of your Majesty's Colonies may be repealed." King George III refused to receive it, angrily condemning Americans as a people in "open and avowed rebellion."

The colonists now began to seriously think about war. The rebel capital of Philadelphia was easily accessible from the Delaware River and Bay, and American forts, batteries and river obstructions called chevaux-de-frises needed to be installed and soldiers recruited. On June 30, 1775, the Articles of War, a set of rules for governing an army, were adopted by Congress. One month later, a law student in Thomas McKean's office, John Parke of Dover, became Delaware's first soldier in the Continental army. Thomas McKean and Caesar Rodney wrote a letter of recommendation for Parke to the newly appointed General Washington, currently stationed outside Boston. Parke, they said, was "an Ensign in the 2nd Battalion of the Militia here, and is desirous of serving his country as a Volunteer under you. He has frequently drawn his pen and is now resolved to draw his sword in support of the American cause."[21] Parke was appointed an assistant quartermaster general.

The Articles of War had been signed without official state or national governments in place. Now the Thirteen Colonies were thrown into the process of developing their own rules, policies and procedures. Tension was palpable, and busy policy makers had minimal sympathy for vulnerable civilians and less patience for Tories and pacifists. In July 1775, the Second Continental Congress explicitly recommended that conscientious objectors make amends by staging relief efforts "in this time of universal calamity."

In response, the Wilmington Monthly Quaker Meeting of July 1775 appointed a committee of five people—including Stanton-area millers Daniel Byrnes and his brother, Caleb—to coordinate a regional effort to send financial assistance to the poor of Boston. Daniel, who was clerk of Wilmington Monthly Meeting, attended the Meeting of Sufferings in Philadelphia as a visitor on July 13. At that meeting, the Quakers were directed to send their money to

John Reynell of Philadelphia or to Samuel Smith of Burlington, the treasurers of Philadelphia Yearly Meeting. By November, area Friends had forwarded £2,000 sterling to the New England Meeting for distribution.

Loyalty to King George III was still the norm. Americans continued to blame Parliament and the king's advisors for the appalling way the colonies were being treated, but by July 1775, there was nervous acceptance of the need for change. In Christiana, Delaware, rabid local Patriots were beginning to demand public statements of apology from those who publicly clung to the ways of the past:

To the Public.

Whereas I have spoken disrespectfully of the general Congress, as well as of those Military Gentlemen who have associated for the defence of the liberties of America, I now take this opportunity of declaring, that my conduct proceeded from the most contracted notions of the British constitution, and of the right of human nature. I am sorry for my guilt, and am ashamed of my folly. I now believe all Assemblies to be legal and constitutional, which are formed by the united suffrages of a free people; and am convinced that no soldiers are so respectable, as those citizens who take up arms in defence of liberty. I believe that Kings are no longer to be feared or obeyed than while they execute just laws; and that a corrupted British Ministry, with a venal Parliament at their heels, are now attempting to reduce the American Colonies to the lowest degree of slavery. I most sincerely wish that the counsels of the Congress may always be directed with wisdom, and that the arms of America may always be crowned with success. And I pray that every man in America, who behaves as I have formerly done, may not meet with the lenity which I have experienced, but may be obliged to expiate his crimes in a more ignominious manner.— Mordechai Levy. *Philadelphia, July 14, 1775*

Whereas I have, some time since, frequently made use of rash and imprudent expressions with respect to the conduct of my worthy Fellow Citizens, who are now engaged in a noble and patriotic struggle against the arbitrary measures of the British ministry, which conduct has justly raised their resentments against me. I now confess that I have acted extremely wrong in so doing, for which I am exceedingly sorry, and humbly ask pardon and forgiveness of the Public; and I do solemnly promise that, for the future, I will conduct myself in such a manner, as to avoid giving any offence: And

*at the same time, in justice to myself, must declare, that I am not unfriendly
to the present Measures pursued by the Friends to American Liberty, but
do heartily approve of them, and as far as is in my power will endeavour
to promote them.—AMOS WICKERSHAM. Philadelphia, July 17, 1775.*[22]

The Continental Congress resolved that "a day of publick humiliation,
fasting, and prayer" be held on Thursday, July 20, 1775, "to bless our
rightful sovereign, King George the Third." The newly elected president of
Congress, John Hancock, instructed the colonists to pray for a resumption
of "the just rights and privileges of the Colonies" in "civil and religious"
matters. Congress attended "Divine Service" and ordered that a copy of the
resolution be "published in the Newspapers, and in Hand-bills."

*This Congress, therefore, considering the present, critical, alarming and
calamitous State of these Colonies, do earnestly recommend that Thursday
the 20ᵗʰ Day of July next, be observed by the Inhabitants of all the English
Colonies on this Continent, as a Day of public Humiliation, Fasting and
Prayer; that we may, with united Hearts and Voices…confess and deplore our
many Sins; and offer up our joint Supplications to the all-wise, omnipotent,
and merciful Disposer of all Events; humbly beseeching him to forgive
our Iniquities, to remove our present Calamities, to avert those desolating
Judgments, with which we are threatened, and to bless our rightful Sovereign
King George the Third, and to inspire him with Wisdom to discern and
pursue the true Interests of his Subjects, that a speedy end may be put to the
civil discord between Great-Britain and the American Colonies.*[23]

Joseph Montgomery, Presbyterian pastor at New Castle, observed
Continental Congress's day of fasting on July 20 with a sermon to the
local militia company. Montgomery began by stressing the powerful
communal nature of the fast day with some "two millions of intelligent
beings…engaged in the same public acts of religious worship," a
"grand Assembly of the inhabitants of the continent…by order of the
Congress." The heart of Montgomery's sermon proclaimed the need for
united action and fused religious and political inspiration. After reading
the proclamation of the Continental Congress, Reverend Montgomery
told the militia that the "fatal day…is come, when our connection with
the parent state must be dissolved."[24]

The New Castle Committee of Inspection criticized resident Alexander
Porter for ordering his slaves to process grain on the day of fasting and prayer.

Porter claimed to have done this based on "an apprehension prevailing in the neighborhood of the Negroes, rising and destroying the white people." By keeping his slaves busy all day, he thought, he had "prevented them from running through the country, putting good people in fear." While admitting that his actions were "apparently contrary" to the resolves of Congress, Porter insisted that his actions marked no opposition to the movement "to free our countrymen in America from a compleat system of slavery."[25]

The word *slavery* was being bandied about a great deal. Although Delaware had outlawed the importation of slaves in 1774, there remained many slave owners in Delaware and elsewhere. Daniel Byrnes defiantly composed an abolitionist tract questioning the warmongers' definition of freedom. Daniel's broadside was marked for release on the day established by the Continental Congress for prayer and fasting. Whether it was printer James Adams of Wilmington or members of the Wilmington Friends Meeting who decided to withhold it from publication until August 4 is unknown. In his broadside, "An Address to the British Colonies in North America," Byrnes

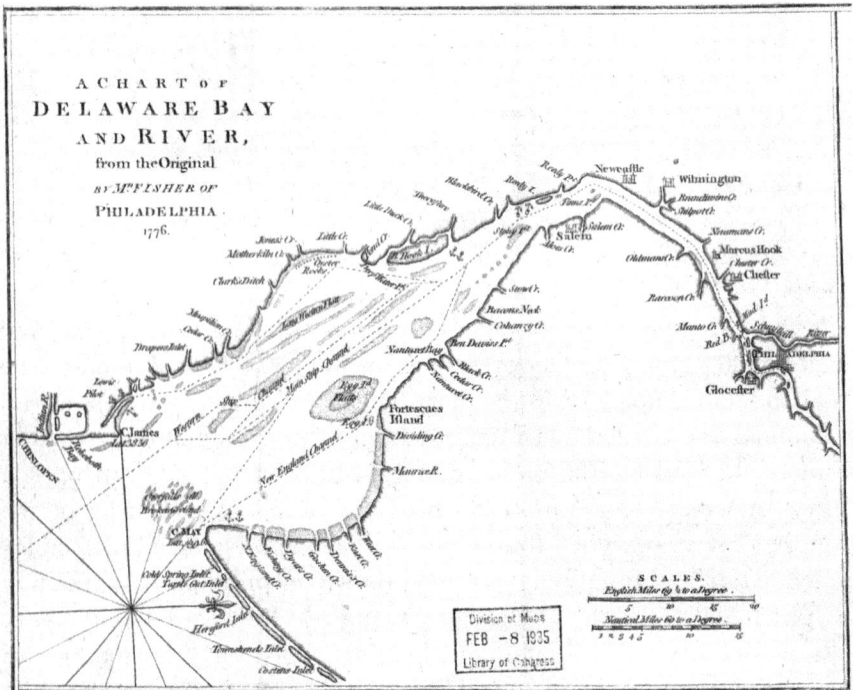

Joshua Fisher's Map, 1776. Nautical chart showing shoals, tidal flats, ship channels, shoreline anchorages and port towns up to Philadelphia. Oriented with north to the right. *Library of Congress.*

boldly asked, "What about those who are truly enslaved?": "Can we be so unwise as to suppose, that a god infinitely just, will be partial in our favor, or that he will hear our prayers, until we have put away the evil of our doings from before his eyes? How can any have the confidence to put up addresses to a god of impartial justice, and ask of him success in a struggle for freedom, who at the same time are keeping others in a state of abject slavery?"[26] Publication of this broadside meant that Byrnes would forever be walking on a tightrope, knowing that by printing and distributing his thoughts there was a very real possibility that he had endangered himself and his family.

In Dover, delegates from all the Lower Three Counties met that month. This Council of Safety would be in charge of confirming the appointment of militia officers, drafting militia regulations and raising and supplying troops, as requested by the Continental Congress. The Dover Committee found Daniel Varnum guilty of using such expressions as, "[H]e had liefe be under a tyrannical king as a tyrannical Commonwealth, especially if the damned Presbyterians had the rule of it," but accepted his recantation.[27]

Chapter 4

ROLLIN' ON THE RIVER

In Philadelphia, on September 19, 1775, Benjamin Franklin, Philip Livingston, Silas Deane, John Alsop, John Langdon, Samuel Ward, John Dickinson, Thomas McKean and Thomas Willing were assigned to the Continental Congress's "Secret Committee," formed for the purpose of obtaining gunpowder and ordnance. Five would be a quorum, and "business [was] conducted with as much secrecy as the nature of the service will possibly admit." McKean was appointed clerk of this committee.[28] Secret Committee minutes for September 27, 1775, reveal the Congress reaching out to Europe for weapons and supplies:

A Contract was enterd into by Thos. Willing & Robert Morris & Co. of the City of Philadelphia in the Province of Pensylva., Merchts of the one part, with Samuel Ward, John Langdon, Silas Deane, John Alsop, Philip Livingston, Benjamin Franklin, John Dickenson & Thos. McKean the aforesaid Members of the other part as follows vizt.—That the sd. Thos. Willing, Robert Morris & Co. shall & will, with the utmost speed & secrecy send a ship or vessel to some part of Europe & there purchase at the cheapest rate they can a thousand barrels of good powder, twelve good brass guns (six pounders), two thousand stand of good arms vizt. Soldiers muskets & bayonets & five thousand gunlocks double bridled, of a good quality, & in case the aforesaid quantity of powder cannot be procurd, that they shall & will purchase as much Saltpetre & sulphur if to be had as will make as much powder as shall be deficient. As by the sd. Contract copied into the Register of the Contracts of the sd. p. 2 &C bearing date the day & year aforesaid, reference being thereunto had, more fully & at large appears.[29]

Life in the Lower Three Counties was reasonably peaceful, but fears were growing that a British naval force would come up the Delaware River before American defense units were ready. Henry Fisher of Lewes was pressed into service to figure out how to alert Philadelphia at the approach of British men-of-war. He was empowered to supervise the river pilots in the lower Delaware Bay, and he helped establish thirteen alarm posts between Lewes and the mouth of Frankford Creek in Pennsylvania. These were Cape Henlopen, Mispillion River, Murderkill River, Bombay Hook, Port Penn, Long Point, Dalby Point (probably near Claymont and Marcus Hook), Chester, Thompson Point, Billingsport, Gloucester, Market Street Wharf and Frankford Creek. From Port Penn north, these stations were equipped with cannons. The lower alarm posts all seem to have had small boats, probably pilot boats, in addition to a three- or four-pounder cannon.

On November 1, 1775, the Continental Congress stated that, with the exception of licensed shipments of military supplies or other congressionally designated purposes, no produce of the United Colonies would be exported until March.[30] In early August, the Continental Congress resolved, "That the Marine Committee be directed to order the ships and armed vessels, belonging to the continent, out on such cruises as they shall think proper," but it was not until December that Esek Hopkins of Rhode Island was appointed commander in chief of the Continental navy. His fleet was to consist of seven ships: two twenty-four-gun frigates, the *Alfred* and the *Columbus*; two fourteen-gun brigs, the *Andrea Doria* and the *Cabot*; and three schooners, the *Hornet*, the *Wasp* and the *Fly*. That winter, the Delaware River froze. Hopkins's fleet was in Philadelphia, waiting for the ice in the river to break up.

Conditions were not suitable for taking Esek Hopkins's fleet downriver until February 11. Fearful that the Continental Naval Committee was "taking the Bread from their mouths," the Delaware River pilots asked Henry Fisher to act as their spokesman. In response, the naval committee approved ten river pilots to serve as pilots and scouts of the waterway, sending dispatches of enemy activity on the coast to Philadelphia throughout the war.[31]

Now the Continental Congress called for the formation of an official Continental army. There had been an organized militia in the Three Lower Counties on Delaware since the days of the French and Indian War, but on December 9, 1775, Congress ordered that the lower counties on Delaware raise a battalion for the Continental army.

1776: YANKEE DOODLE, MIND THE STEP

On January 1, 1776, "a call was made to arms." Among the first to sign up were Delawareans Peter Jaquett[32] and Robert Kirkwood, both of whom would fight until the end of the war. By January 21, the Delaware Council of Safety had completed its list of commissioned officers and staff officers. Colonel John Haslet's name was at the top of the roster of field and staff officers, with Gunning Bedford as lieutenant colonel, Thomas McDonough as major, Reverend Joseph Montgomery as chaplain, Dr. James Tilton as surgeon, Robert Ballas quartermaster and Thomas Holland as adjutant.[33]

One of the private soldiers, Samuel Lockwood, later wrote about his experiences:

> [A]t Lewestown, Sussex County, state of Delaware, early in the beginning of the year 1776, the precise day nor month not now recollected but thinks it must have been in January or February of that year and served under Capt. David Hall, afterward Colonel Hall...as a private soldier for about three or four months, alternatively guarding at the lighthouse which was on Cape Henlopen (about the distance of one mile from Lewestown) and working on the fort at Lewestown. That is to say, a portion of the troops was at stated times detailed from their usual duties in the camp and taken on what was called fatigue duty, which was to work as aforesaid and any other work which was necessary to put the country along the shore of the bay in a state of defense. He continued engaged as before stated and under the officers before named until about May or June, the month not now precisely recollected, when he was transferred to another regiment...This whole year was occupied by the company to which he belonged by guarding at the lighthouse and working as aforesaid, always taking their muskets, etc., with them. And whenever they heard two cannons (which was the signal), they laid by their laboring tools, seized their arms, and repaired to

A View of the Lighthouse on Cape Henlopen, Taken at Sea, August 1780. Illustration in the *Columbian Magazine, or Monthly Miscellany*, Philadelphia. Printed for Seddon, Spotswood, Cist and Trenchard, February 1788. *Library of Congress.*

the point where there was danger apprehended and again, when the alarm was over, returned to their work unless the time for their relief had arrived.[34]

By March 3, 1776, Andrew Snape Hamond, captain of the British warship, *Roebuck*, had been tasked with establishing British naval control on the Delaware. He needed additional troops to operate on both the Delaware and New Jersey sides of the river and bemoaned the lack of success in hiring a river pilot from Cape Henlopen. He asked Parliament for more ships, some hand mortars and a few howitzers, which could fire both bombs and cannonballs.

On March 27, the Philadelphia Committee of Safety, in charge of all the river fortifications above Wilmington, received word from Henry Fisher of Lewes that the forty-four-gun frigate *Roebuck* and a tender had entered the mouth of the Delaware Bay. The committee immediately ordered four row galleys to report to the American brigantine *Lexington*, under the command of Captain John Barry,[35] and to "exert their utmost endeavors to take or destroy all such vessels of the enemy as they might find in the Delaware."[36] As a result, Captain Lawrence with the *Salamander* and Captain Hause with the guard boat *Eagle* were sent to Lewes. The *Eagle* and supplies were to be placed at Fisher's disposal. Upon their arrival, Fisher was handed a letter from the naval committee. Unhappy about an official order prohibiting him from using his pilots as the crew of the *Eagle*, he wrote back that his pilots were of a different character from those employed in Philadelphia, and "as the Boat is to be stationed at our Creeks mouth I cannot see there will be the least danger in letting six pilots go in her and the remainder Landsmen as the pilots are acquainted with the great gun and they can always see their danger before they can be suppressed."[37]

Colonel John Haslet deployed two companies of his Delaware battalion to Lewes. On April 7, 1776, a skirmish ensued south of Lewes in which a merchant ship was attacked by one of the *Roebuck*'s tenders. Gunfire from the Delaware Continental Regiment and cannon fire from the merchant ship helped keep the *Roebuck*'s tender and crew from any further attempts. Haslet reported to George Read that he had *Roebuck*'s third lieutenant and three soldiers in custody. They had been taken from a tender at about four o'clock in the morning after "the helmsman fell asleep [and] Providence steered the boat ashore." Haslet said that he would keep the men in custody until Congress "directs what to do." Scharf's *History of Delaware* noted, "This spirited little skirmish…[removed] from the minds of the patriots the exaggerated impression of the invincibility of the British ships and sailors, and they flocked to the shores of the bay in readiness for another encounter."[38]

By mid-April, eight of the thirteen delegations in Philadelphia had received instructions from home to vote in favor of independence should a resolution to that effect be offered. New York, New Jersey, Pennsylvania, Delaware and Maryland were the five colonies that were not ready to declare for separation. With armed British ships battling in the river, that was perhaps not too surprising.

On May 5, the *Roebuck* sailed up Delaware Bay with the *Liverpool*, a British frigate carrying twenty-eight guns and a number of tenders and prizes. Two days later, Colonel Haslet wrote to Caesar Rodney from Cantwell's Bridge that he had received a message that the *Roebuck* and *Liverpool* were off the coast of Port Penn and moving north toward New Castle. The British ships soon established a position between the mouth of the Christiana and Chester, Pennsylvania.

On the afternoon of May 8, 1776, thirteen Pennsylvania row galleys, aided by the six-gun Continental schooner *Wasp*—which came out from Christiana Creek where it had been forced by the British—attacked the enemy ships anchored below Chester. According to an account in a Philadelphia paper, a heavy exchange of fire continued for three or four hours, drawing a crowd

River pilot's house. The house was built in 1739 and sold to Luke Shields Sr., a Delaware Bay and Delaware River pilot in 1741. The Thomas Maull House has been restored by and is owned and operated by the Colonel David Hall Chapter, NSDAR. *Delaware Public Archives and Denise Clemmons.*

Heron. Bombay Hook. *Karen Sinar Dever.*

of thousands to the riverbanks to watch. At dusk, the *Roebuck* ran aground in shallow water, and the *Liverpool* was forced to anchor nearby to protect it until the firing stopped after dark. The next day, May 9, the *Roebuck* floated off the bar on which it had foundered the night before, and the American row galleys resumed their attack. Firing constantly, the Americans chased the British ships six miles back down the river to New Castle, where they moored for the night.

Perceptions of the naval battle differed. Colonel Samuel Miles sourly wrote to the Pennsylvania Committee of Safety, "I believe there is no damage done on either side, tho' I suppose three or four hundred shot have passed between them…our boats in my opinion engage at too great a distance…a great deal of ammunition has been wasted."[39]

William Barry, an American prisoner on the *Roebuck*, reported that it received

> *many shots betwixt the wind and water: some went quite through, some in her quarter, and was much raked fore and aft…one man was killed by a shot…Six were much hurt and burned by an eighteen-pound cartridge of powder taking fire, among whom was an acting lieutenant, and several were hurt by splinters…During the engagement, the Captain ordered several of the guns to be loaded with round and grape shot…the carpenters…having taken…forty of the row galleys' balls out of the "Roebuck," and some cannot be come at.*[40]

Snape Hamond's own version was that "[w]e met them under sail and lay under the disadvantage of being obliged to engage them at the distance they chose to fix on, which was scarcely within point blank shot: and being such low objects on the water, it was with some difficulty that we could strike them, so that we fired upon them near two hours before they thought proper to retire, and row off."[41]

George Read wrote to Caesar Rodney pleading for more powder and lead for the troops at Lewes. Read was "well satisfied" with the row galleys, noting that "they have produced a very happy effect on the multitudes of spectators on each side of the river."

Snape Hamond's official report merely noted, "After having fully executed what I had in view, I returned to the Capes the 15th."[42]

In spite of ship battles in the river, the Three Lower Counties on Delaware squabbled about the need for a change in government recommended by Congress that day. Allen McLane from Duck Creek, Smyrna, later identified June 1776 as the "date of decision," a time when

Dover Green. *Delaware Public Archives.*

everyone had to choose the side on which to stand. "When the question [of independence] was first agitated in the committees a considerable majority was opposed to the measure," he claimed. "The few Whigs (and very few indeed) became desperate, dreaded the consequence of being captured and treated as rebels."

Reasoned debate once again occasionally gave way to violence. "[Patriots] attacked the disaffected with tar and feathers, rotten eggs…and succeeded in silencing the disaffected and then filling those committees with men determined to be free."[43] Ordinary courtesies and customs seemed to have been forgotten.

Chapter 5

CHOCK-FULL OF LIES
AND STORIES

Paranoia was growing. Loyalist Thomas Robinson was traveling to the General Assembly meeting when Dover militia officers stopped him and threatened him with jail. After his colleague Jacob Moore drew his sword at them, offering to defend Robinson's life, both men were jailed. Kent County members of the assembly urged for their immediate release. In September 1775, Moore had, in fact, been appointed colonel in command of a battalion of Sussex County Militia.

Like Thomas Robinson, Dover's Vincent Loockerman fit the standard profile of a Loyalist almost perfectly. He was a wealthy Anglican, engaged in overseas trade and made his home in southern Delaware, a place where social unrest instigated by Tories was never far from the government's concerns. His family, with connections in shipping and trade from Philadelphia to London and Bristol, could not ignore the growing conflict. In spite of potential Loyalist leanings, Vincent Loockerman Jr. joined the Militia Light Infantry Company of Dover under Thomas Rodney, and according to a note in Thomas Rodney's private log, he brought his own gun "in good order." On May 12, Thomas Rodney wrote, "Loockerman is frightened almost out of his wits & seems half at least on the other side of the question—his late conduct has been so particularly penurious that he is abused by almost everybody—There was much fun with him last night but it is too long to tell."

Both Vincent Loockerman Jr. and his father served as members of the Delaware Assembly for several terms. As early as July 1775, Loockerman Sr. was one of the people involved in choosing the design of the flags that would be used by Delaware's troops. Caesar Rodney asked his brother in Dover to "assure Mr. Loockerman they will be ellegant and cleaver [*sic*]." Two years later, with the Delaware Continental Regiment desperately in need of new clothing, he lent the State of Delaware £750, half of the amount the Delaware legislature had approved as bills of credit to support the troops during the war.[44]

In June 1776, Whigs circulated a petition calling for a Delaware constitutional convention. Tories immediately circulated a counter-petition, which may have been written by Thomas Robinson. As John Clark of Kent County was on his way to present the Tory document to Congress, he was seized and put in the pillory and his petition destroyed. In June 1776, Thomas Rodney told the story best in the form of a rollicking song:

"LIGHT HORSE MONDAY/BLACK MONDAY"

CHORUS
Black Munday was a mighty day
For refugees and Tories
Three hundred bravely ran away
Chock full of lies and stories
Lang do Lang Diddle

The Captain of the brave light Horse
Began the insurrection
His Videts flew on every course
To spread the wide infection
Lang do Lang Diddle

Dark and Secret was their plan
To burn the Town of Dover
But e're their furious work began
They were all quite don Over
Lang do Lang Diddle

Tidings came about Midnight
The Town would be invaded
And the Infantry 'er Morning light
Like Lyons all paraded
Lang do Lang Diddle

For Satan first the standard rear'd
Of impious Insurrection
And to him Each Evil mind repair'd
Who caught the foul infection
Lang do Lang Diddle

He was ever deemed tence
The Prince of proud Rebell'on
And all insurgents hurried since
With all their crimes to Hellon
Lang do Lang Diddle

Tidings came they were undone
Their Captain was arrested
Their impious plans were all made known
And all their crimes detested
Lang do Lang Diddle

In spite of the insurrection in Dover, thirty delegates met in the courthouse in New Castle on June 15, 1776. These men unanimously decided that the Lower Three Counties on the Delaware were to be free not only from Britain but also from governance by the Penn family. They would form their own state government. After dismissing Governor John Penn, Caesar Rodney, Speaker of the Delaware Assembly, would be the state's highest-ranking officer. If the Americans lost the Revolution, Rodney, McKean and Read, as well as all other Delaware colonial leaders, knew that they would be accused of treason against Britain.

With warships already prowling the new state's eastern border, many Delawareans considered the assembly's decision to be both stupid and dangerous. Caesar Rodney had to immediately leave New Castle for Sussex County to deal with Tory protests. William Adair, a resident of Sussex County, noted in his diary, "June 19–20. Colonel Rodney came to try Tories with 1,000 men viz Colonel John Haslet's Battalion, also a fair representation of riflemen to reduce a Tory insurrection here. Witnesses examined for four days. Tories ordered to bring in their arms and ammunition." On June 23–25, he wrote, "Robinson, Manlove, and Ingram fled to Somerset, are raising an insurrection at Snow Hill."[45] This situation was too precarious for Caesar Rodney to leave Sussex County, even though he was due in Philadelphia on July 1.

Chapter 6

THE DECLARATION
OF INDEPENDENCE

T he Declaration of Independence was a product of the Second
Continental Congress. Two earlier intercolonial conferences had
occurred, each building toward colonial unity. The Stamp Act Congress
and the First Continental Congress had brought greater participation from
the Thirteen Colonies. Each time the representatives met, they were more
accustomed to compromising and talking to one another.

Without Caesar Rodney's presence in Philadelphia, Delaware's vote on
the Declaration of Independence was tied—Thomas McKean voting for
and George Read against. A second and final vote would be taken the next
day. McKean angrily sent a rider at his personal expense to find Caesar
Rodney. The message reached Rodney in Dover around midnight. Whether
Rodney arrived in a carriage or on horseback, as legend has it, he arrived
at Independence Hall the next afternoon. Rodney wrote to his brother,
Thomas, that he had arrived "in time Enough to give my Voice in the matter
of Independence."[46]

Today, we have largely forgotten that the Declaration of Independence
was a formal declaration of an ongoing war. When the Declaration came
back from the printers, and those who had voted "aye" signed it, George
Read added his name, but John Dickinson, voting for Pennsylvania,
declined. A letter from John Haslet to Caesar Rodney shows an offhand
acceptance of the Declaration. The pressing issues close at hand were
topmost in his mind:

Five-man drafting committee presenting their draft of the Declaration of Independence to the Continental Congress on June 28, 1776, not the signing of the document, which took place later. John Trumbull, artist, 1817. *Library of Congress.*

Lewes. July 6, 1776

I was embarrassed by the order of Congress directing two companies to Cape May. I hope to receive your answer by this day's post.

Last Monday Evening arrived here Gen Dagworthy, Jones, and a band of patriots from Broad-Creek, who dispose and say an open correspondence is carried on for the purpose of trade with Lord Dunmore, that he daily visits his scattered bands among them; that Tories seem rather irritated than reformed. A copy of their depositions is enclosed...I have ordered down one company of the Delaware and...a copy of my orders to the officer who commands the detachment is enclosed to you, and I would hope my tardiness in obeying [the] Cape May order will not be supposed to originate in any other principle than mentioned in my last to you. For God's sake, let us have arms. May we not have those saved by Captain Barry from the Brig? Will it not be in your power to engage for us [enough to] complete one company now Pennsylvania is supplied?

I congratulate you, Sir, on the Important Day, which restores to Every American his Birthright! A Day which every freeman will record with gratitude and the millions of Posterity with Rapture. Ensign Wilson arrived here last night… [a fine] *feast at Dover anticipated, and announced the Declaration of Congress. Even the Barrister himself laid aside his airs of reserve, mighty happy. I must beg pardon for having taken up so much of your time with small matters.*

I am with great esteem and respect,

Yr John Haslet.[47]

In Lewes two weeks later, Haslet's Delaware Continental Regiment celebrated with a reading of the Declaration of Independence, three cannon blasts and three toasts. In Dover, Kent County officials threw an image of George III into a bonfire with this exclamation: "Compelled by strong necessity thus we destroy even the shadow of that king who refused to reign over a free people." In New Castle, at the end of the month, nearly

Old Saint Anne's Episcopal Church, Middletown, Delaware. *Delaware Public Archives.*

five hundred cheering Patriots witnessed a reading of the Declaration and a bonfire fueled by the king's arms. Lieutenant Enoch Anderson of Newport, Delaware, later recalled, "We took out of the Court House all the insignia of the monarchy—all the baubles of Royalty and made a pile of them before the Court House, set fire to them and burnt them to ashes. This was our first jubilee…and a merry day we made of it."[48]

On July 28 (some say in response to pleas, not to mention the obligatory Anglican prayers for the king), Reverend Philip Reading, who had come from England in 1746, told his congregation at St. Anne's Parish in Middletown to keep the faith and then locked the church. Father Reading died in 1778, but St. Anne's was not reopened until the war ended several years later.[49]

Only a few weeks after the Declaration of Independence was signed, the Delaware Continental Regiment received orders to march to Philadelphia. By August 3, 1776, the entire regiment of approximately eight hundred men was in Philadelphia, where it was supplied with equipment and imported muskets.[50]

BATTLE OF BROOKLYN

Toward the end of the month, word came that the British army had landed on Long Island, hoping to divide the rebellious colonies in half by gaining control of the Hudson River. On August 27, 1776, American general William Alexander, Lord Stirling, positioned the Delaware and Maryland regiments on a rise of land between Eighteenth and Twentieth Streets to defend the most direct route from the British landing site to the American fortifications in Brooklyn Heights. Twice attacking a much larger force, this group succeeded delaying the enemy. Although the Delaware and Maryland troops faced the fiercest fighting of the day, they held their ground, allowing the remainder of Washington's army to retreat to the safety of the fortifications. Haslet reported two privates killed, two officers killed and twenty-three missing. Caesar Rodney, in a letter to George Read dated September 4, stated that the Delaware battalion lost thirty-one men in this battle.[51]

SOCIETY OF FRIENDS

Many Delawareans were Quakers, whose ancestors had come to America early in William Penn's administration. Even those who had disagreed with England's policies were having a hard time reconciling the changes in the air with their religious beliefs and good business sense. As the news filtered home from the soldiers in New York, a schism occurred among Delaware members of the Society of Friends.[52]

Worried that their homes and families might be threatened, many men and boys felt that they should join the war effort. Although the basic tenet of the Quaker faith is pacifism, Wilmington Friends Meeting's records are full of very specific admonitions, such as the following:

> *Minutes: Whereas Jacob Bennett,[53] son of Joseph Bennett has had a birthright amongst the people called Quakers but by not taking heed to the peaceable principles we has so far…the good order established amongst us as to join the…to learn the art of war and as Friends having treated with him in order to reclaim him has not had the desired object therefore for clearing Truth and our society from such disorder by members, we declare the said Jacob Bennett no member with us until he by repentance and…Signed in and on behalf of the Monthly Meeting of Friends…at Wilmington the 17th 9th Mo. 1776 by Daniel Byrnes, Clerk.[54]*

George Washington recommended that a reservist or home guard be created because it could be highly mobile and ready to move quickly to wherever it was needed. Known as the "Flying Camp," it was to be composed of militia units from New Jersey, Pennsylvania, Delaware and Maryland under the command of Brigadier General Hugh Mercer of Virginia. Samuel Patterson, a miller from Christiana Bridge, Delaware, was appointed battalion colonel. The Flying Camp's job would be to guard the vulnerable coastline, protect the Continental army's supply lines, suppress roving bands of Tories and act as a ready reserve should Washington have need of reinforcements.[55]

The men recruited for the Flying Camp were to be based in New Jersey, with militiamen from three colonies: six thousand from Pennsylvania, thirty-four thousand from Maryland and six hundred from Delaware. They were to serve until December 1, 1776, unless discharged sooner by Congress, and were to be paid and fed in the same manner as regular soldiers of the Continental army. On September 19, Samuel Patterson wrote to George Read Sr., "Yesterday five companies went off by water. Captain Latimer today; and what few remained of Captain Woodgate's yesterday had they all paraded to embark. The whole almost lay down their arms, swore they would not go without a bounty such as others got in Pennsylvania."[56]

Meanwhile, another entire company deserted in the night. Patterson blamed lower officers chosen by their own men, claiming that they "sacrifice Liberty to licentiousness." In spite of these squabbles, Delaware supplied roughly 460 out of a requested 600 men to the Flying Camp.[57]

Chapter 7

FUNNY MONEY
AND OTHER PROBLEMS

The new nation, having just broken away from the mother country, had no cash reserves. Paper currency was printed, but laws, penalties, entreaties and the most enduring patriotism could not sustain the value of Continental currency backed by nothing but the promise of "future tax revenues." Businessmen, Quakers among others, felt that this new paper money had little or no value and refused to accept it in trade. Reasons for opposition included: paper money led to inflation and therefore depreciated in value; using the currency was a political statement endorsing an "authority whose legitimacy the Society of Friends did not acknowledge"; and the money was raised to fund the war effort.

George Washington grumbled, "A wagonload of currency will hardly purchase a wagonload of provisions." Ultimately, the Continental currency failed and left the young nation saddled with a hefty war debt.

The Society of Friends instructed members to avoid participating in anything that might contribute to the war, including political service and the circulation of paper money. John Cowgill, a Quaker from central Delaware, refused Continental currency on this principle and was arrested and paraded through the streets with a sign on his back declaring, "On the circulation of the Continental currency depends the fate of America."[58]

In the autumn of 1776, Delaware's state constitution was approved and elections held.[59] Election results from each of Delaware's three counties were reported. The *Minutes of the Council of the Delaware State* were first recorded on October 28, 1776. An upper house of nine members, called the Legislative

Council, and a lower house of twenty-one members, known as the House of Assembly, would now govern the little state. In joint session, the two houses chose a president who would have a three-year term, governing with the assistance of a four-man Privy Council. Under this new constitution, officials already in office, except for Governor Penn, continued to perform their duties. The two houses divided the legislative power. The structure provided by the new constitution was cumbersome and frequently inefficient, but its most notable provision urged the banning of importation of slaves from Africa or elsewhere.[60]

In late September and early October, Thomas McKean went to Philadelphia, where the Congressional Secret Committee was empowered to take such measures as it deemed necessary for the purchasing and arming of a frigate and two cutters, with the expectation that the frigate would make "a cruise in the British channel against our enemy." Around the tenth, McKean, a radical Whig, returned to New Castle to campaign for the Delaware election. On October 21, he was elected to the new, mostly moderate and conservative Delaware Assembly. McKean wrote to his wife, "I arrived about dark the day I left you, and am well. Mr. Read is Speaker of the Council and Mr. McKinly of the Assembly—they were both chosen before I got down." Much of the time of this legislative body was devoted to adjusting the old governmental structure to the new state constitution. McKean, Robinson and Ridgely were appointed as a committee for enlisting a Delaware battalion to join the service of the United States.

Between October 11 and 21, 1776, an epidemic hit the Flying Camp—3 of Samuel Patterson's men died, and 70 were sick.[61] On October 22, Haslet's Delaware Continental Regiment fought in a nighttime attack against the Queen's Rangers led by Robert Rogers (of French and Indian War fame) at Mamaroneck, New York. They captured 36 men and a collection of weapons and blankets. On October 25, with about 280 men still fit for duty, the regiment took part in the Battle of White Plains. Haslet's men defended Chatterton's Hill, retreating only as the American forces did. After the loss of Forts Washington and Lee in November, the American army withdrew from New York into New Jersey, with British troops in pursuit. Haslet's men again guarded the rear of the army as the Americans crossed the Delaware into Pennsylvania. Read's brother-in-law, Gunning Bedford, wrote, "It was a hard campaign and a discouraging one."[62]

On November 1, Samuel Patterson wrote to George Read from the Flying Camp:

Dear Sir:

Yesterday morning I had orders from Lord Sterling to evacuate my post at Amboy with the troops there—about five hundred men—and the remainder of the stores, cattle, etc., and to join him about three miles off. This I did by sunrise, and then proceeded, with the main body, to Brunswick, where we arrived about two o'clock the whole about nine thousand men, with a good train. But this place is miserably dirty—Many of our men lay out without even tents—most distressing to the campaign and future success of recruiting. Our men many of them sick, hardly a place to put their heads in. Here are Generals Washington, Putnam, Mercer, Green, Stevens, and Beal with their brigades. General Washington has wanted the "flying camp" to stay two weeks, but such proposal will not do with any. I do not much wonder at this, as no place many times to put their heads in. We must do better for the future, or give up our army. Was I in Philadelphia, and an inhabitant, I should remain, in my opinion, secure this winter. Colonel Bedford is here, very poorly, but I think mending; is pleurisy.

I am in haste, yours, etc., Samuel Patterson.[63]

When George Washington Crossed the Delaware

When the terms of the Flying Camp expired in early December, George Read Sr. bemoaned that the men "have left the General in whole brigades… tho' ever more wanted in the field."[64] Enlistments were to run out at the end of the year, and Colonel Haslet had ordered many of his officers to go back to Delaware to begin the recruiting process once more.

The British advance from New York to the Delaware River had a chilling effect on Patriots. Recognizing that his army was dispirited and fading, Washington decided on a bold move to reinvigorate his men. He organized a strike into New Jersey to surprise and capture the garrison of British-held Trenton. The New Castle Militia had displayed some interest in going to Trenton, but the men were unwilling to sign up for six weeks when no provision for pay or other necessary supplies had been mentioned. Part of Kent County's militia stepped up to the task. Thomas Rodney's journal explained their decision:

Washington Crossing the Delaware, Evening Previous to the Battle of Trenton, Dec. 25th, 1776. T. Sully, artist. Etched by W. Humphrys and engraved by G.S. Lang, 1825. *Library of Congress.*

> *Congress had determined to move from Philadelphia to Baltimore...I felt my mind anxious and uneasy, and went over to my brother* [Caesar Rodney] *and he was much concerned; said everything appeared gloomy and unfortunate...When I left him, I consulted the* [militia] *officers and several of the company, and they voluntarily agreed to turn out...And thirty-five of the infantry, including several others, entered into the association to go, and this company marched from Dover the 14th of December 1776 at 3 o'clock in the afternoon.*[65]

In response to Washington's request, thirty-five Kent County militiamen marched north from Dover on the afternoon of December 14, 1776, stopping at Duck Creek (now Smyrna) and meeting up with the baggage wagon and Caesar Rodney's younger brother, Thomas Rodney, at the Trap (McDonough). Their march continued through Red Lion and Christiana, where they stopped at Samuel Patterson's to be fitted out with knapsacks, canteens and more. They then continued past Wilmington to Philadelphia and beyond, joining Washington's army in Bucks County, Pennsylvania. Rodney noted that the road along the way was "full of citizens from Philadelphia, who had fled with their families and effects, expecting the British army would be there in a few days."

In his diary, Rodney described Washington's crossing:

> *Our light Infantry Battalion* [composed of the Dover company and four companies of Philadelphia militia under Captain George Henry] *were embarked in boats to cover the landing of the Brigade. When we reached the Jersey shore we were obliged to land on the ice, 150 yards from the shore. The River was also very full of floating ice and the wind was blowing very hard, and the night was very dark and cold, and we had great difficulty in crossing but the night was very favorable to the enterprise...About 600 of the light troops got over...there was so much floating rain and sleet, and there was so much floating ice in the River that we had the greatest difficulty to get over again, and some of our men did not get over that night. As soon as I reached the Pennsylvania shore I received orders to march to our quarters, where I arrived a little before daylight very*

Washington at Princeton, January 3, 1777. D. Brückner, artist. D. McLellan, lithographer, 26 Spruce Street, New York. Colonel John Haslet (1727–1777) of Milford, Delaware, was killed at the Battle of Princeton on January 3, 1777. *Library of Congress.*

cold... [On the twenty-sixth] *about 12 o'clock the remainder of my company came in, and in the evening we heard of General Washington's success at Trenton and that he had captured 900 Hessians.*[66]

In the course of the crossing, the Delaware Continental Regiment's Colonel John Haslet fell in the icy river but managed to cross, marching ten miles through the wintry blasts to fight the Hessian troops garrisoned in Trenton.

Lieutenant Enoch Anderson of Newport, Delaware, observed with pride, "Our Regiment, although many of the men's enlistments were up, stuck to." The Continentals came back across the river to the Pennsylvania side on December 27, 1776, and the soldiers began to go home. By the end of Delaware's enlistment term, December 31, 1776, only Colonel Haslet, two other officers, a surgeon, two privates and some of Thomas Rodney's Kent County Militia remained. John Haslet was killed on January 3, 1777, at the Battle of Princeton.

1777

Activity in the Delaware River and Bay area continued. A member of the House of Assembly received a message from Jacob Bennett (who had been admonished by the Wilmington Friends Meeting the previous September for joining the war effort) that he had been taken by a British ship of war to the southward of Cape Henlopen and there saw five persons arrive in a boat with some livestock for the British. Bennett claimed that one of these was Daniel Dingee, a member of the House of Assembly. Being informed that John Trip and Levi Potter were prisoners at the same time, a summons was issued to Jacob Bennett, John Trip and Levi Potter to attend the next council meeting, on January 17 at 11:00 a.m., to give evidence. The Speaker of the assembly, with a number of the members of that house, and Mr. Dingee attended the hearing. The council decided that the accusations were groundless and "ordered that Mr. Dingee take his seat as a member of this body."[67]

The next public officials accused of cooperating with the British did not escape censure. On January 27, 1777, the house resumed, and orders for arresting Boas Manlove and Thomas Robinson of the county were read and laid on the table. Minutes from the February 18 meeting of the assembly noted that Boas Manlove, late of Sussex County, "doth retain in his hands the sum of three hundred and eighty pounds, part of the Sussex County quota of the Bills of Credit ordered to be emitted by an Act of Assembly that had been deposited in his hands as one of the signers of the bills."[68] In March, after evading several arrests, Manlove, with fellow Tories Thomas Robinson and John F. Smyth, fled to the British ship *Preston*, moored in the Delaware Bay.

That month, John McKinly of Wilmington became the president of Delaware. Thomas Rodney wrote to Caesar Rodney that the Delaware Assembly had been "very exact in their choice as he [McKinly] is the only man that could so fully represent the Whig and Tory complexion of the State." David Hall of Lewes, who had served as captain in the 1st Delaware under Colonel John Haslet at the Battles of Long Island and White Plains, was now asked to lead the Delaware Continental Regiment.

In Philadelphia, the Pennsylvania Executive Committee, in cooperation with the Continental Congress, made a survey of the Pennsylvania side of the river, making special note of places where the enemy might land. The survey—ordered to be done "with as much secrecy and dispatch as the nature of it will admit" so that Tories would not learn of it—was to extend "down the river as far as Christina Creek" in Delaware. Blocking the Delaware River below Philadelphia began with the construction of a series of underwater obstacles called chevaux-de-frises, as well as the construction of forts at Billingsport and Red Bank in New Jersey and, in the middle of the river itself, Fort Mifflin on Mud Island.

The British warships *Liverpool* and *Roebuck* had been patrolling the river and bay for a long time, but in early April, the Continental Congress advised Delaware to prepare for an attack. In response, the Delaware Assembly was moved away from the river at New Castle to Dover. State president John McKinly asked Caesar Rodney to "plan a guard at Lewes Town…to protect the persons employed as pilots & such property of the good subjects of the United States." On April 10, English men-of-war were in the bay, and on the following day, a volunteer in the Delaware Militia, Samuel Lockwood, witnessed an encounter between the *Roebuck* with British sixth-rate ship the *Perseus* and American ship the *Morris*.[69]

On June 4, Sussex County resident William Adair noted in his diary, "*Roebuck* blowed off her guns in ye road, 2 ships came up the Bay." On the ninth, "The ships blowed off their guns today." In July, he added, "Tories have robbed ten cattle in Mr. Kollock's vessel, clothing, houses at Indian River."[70]

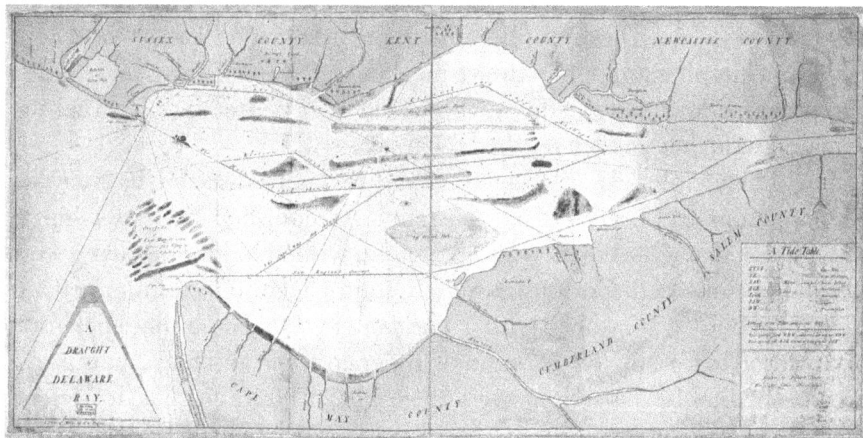

Title on verso: *Delaware River from Capt. Hamond*, 1770. Scale about 1:127,000. Manuscript, pen-and-ink and watercolor. Oriented with north toward the lower right. Depths shown by soundings. Shows ship channels. *Library of Congress.*

On July 21, 1777, a fleet of 261 British ships arrived in the Delaware Bay. A British account noted:

> [A]*ccording to the imbarcation list, there were onboard twenty-seven battalions of British and eight of foreigners; one regiment of light dragoons; a detachment of Artillery, consisting of British riflemen, the Queen's rangers and four comp. of Pioneers. The wind being unfavorable, the fleet did not sail till the 23rd; and on the 28th we were close in with the southern cape* [Henlopen]*; which we imagined we were to run up immediately, but the Roebuck man of war came down from her station there and spoke to the admiral* [Lord Richard Howe] *which seemed to occation* [sic] *a delay.*[71]

After discussions with Captain Andrew Snape Hamond of the *Roebuck* about the Patriots' obstructions in the Delaware River below Philadelphia, Admiral Howe's ships headed south into the Chesapeake Bay, arriving at Head of Elk more than one month later on August 25.

In spite of the activity along the coastline, Delaware Quakers questioned the buzz words "freedom and liberty for all" and grumbled about the political hypocrisy of Americans claiming that they were being "treated like slaves." In the summer of 1775, Daniel Byrnes, clerk of Wilmington Friends Meeting, had published one of America's earliest abolitionist tracts. Now, in May 1777, John Dickinson became the first Founding Father to free his slaves. Dickinson manumitted twelve men and ten women and their children and provided for other children, who would later be freed, to be taught to read and write before they reached the age of ten.

The Philadelphia Yearly Meeting had formally directed its member congregations to observe strict neutrality. Admonished by leadership to suffer in silence, Quaker men and boys who wished to join the army were sternly reprimanded. Curiously enough, John Dickinson was among those who needed to be "reasoned with." The son of a Quaker family, Dickinson had refused to sign the Declaration of Independence and had manumitted his slaves, but he also supported the right of free citizens to defend themselves from direct attack. He had served as chairman of Pennsylvania's Committee of Safety and Defense, organizing the first battalion of troops raised in Philadelphia (today's 111th Infantry, Pennsylvania Army National Guard). When the British entered Delaware in 1777, Dickinson quickly joined the Kent County Militia.

Wilmington Friends Meeting records show a number of Quakers trying to join the war effort.

> *Whereas Moses Patterson who hath made profession and a right of membership with us the people called Quakers hath so far deviated from any peaceable principal as to appear under arms in company with a number of people who were assembled in a martial manner and at another time, joined with others in encouraging military proceedings and on being treated with from time to time on the doctrine he does not appear capable to condemn the said conduct; therefore we do hereby testify against the same and disown him from membership with us as a religious society until he […] his error therein and through repentance be enabled to condemn it to the satisfaction of this meeting, which we sincerely desire he may. Given forth this day by Wilmington Friends Meeting, 28th June 1777.*[72]

Chapter 8

SEIZED IN SEPTEMBER

The Philadelphia Campaign

Although the Delaware Continental Regiment was posted elsewhere, Wilmington's Quaker Hill was full of military activity and soldiers. Soldier William Hutchinson of Chester County wrote:

In the month of July, 1777, and near the latter end of the month, I again joined the army as a volunteer in a company commanded by Capt. Allen Cunningham of New London Crossroads, Chester County, which was about to take the field. We marched the first day to Wilmington, Delaware and were lodged that night in the academy. Next morning proceeded to Chester, at which place our company was lodged in the courthouse and continued there until the main army under the command of General Washington came from Philadelphia on their march to meet the enemy….Next day, after the main army passed through Chester, our captain with his command, agreeably to orders, marched back to Wilmington. Our company were then ordered to work on a hill in the rear of the town in the construction of a fascine battery, at which we continued to work for either three or four days and were then ordered to the banks of Red Clay Creek and were employed in cutting timber to create all possible obstructions in the public roads and highways for the purpose of preventing the passage of the enemy in their march to Philadelphia, which it was generally understood was their design and destination. From Red Clay we passed through Chester County…

[In August and September] *I frequently saw also the Marquis Lafayette and by him we had the honor of being reviewed on Quaker Hill at*

Wilmington, Delaware, while we were at work erecting the battery I have before spoken of and were there addressed by him. He was with us both on horseback and on foot.[73]

Tension escalated. On August 13, 1777, Wilmington Friends Meeting appointed John Perry, John Milhous, Robert Johnson, David Ferris, Joseph West, Daniel Byrnes, Benjamin Hough, Joseph Chambers and Vincent Bonsall to serve as "a Committee to give advice to those who may be in trouble and to collect an account of the sufferings of friends." The committee was to meet monthly.

On August 25, an estimated sixteen thousand British soldiers were unloaded at Head of Elk and began crossing into Delaware, plundering food and supplies on the way. Word from the Continental Congress arrived that Delaware militiamen were to rendezvous at Newport and Christiana Bridge, where they were "to wait the orders of General Washington." In response, eleven thousand American soldiers came south into Delaware from Pennsylvania. The American cavalry pushed on to Wilmington accompanied by George Washington, who established his headquarters at 303 West Street on Quaker Hill.

The following day, Washington and his two principal subordinates, General Nathanael Greene and the Marquis de Lafayette, pushed westward in a torrential downpour to Iron Hill to scope out the enemies' activities. They stayed overnight at the home of Robert Alexander, a Maryland Loyalist. Washington later wrote to Landon Carter, "Not in the dangerous situation you have been led to believe. I was reconnoitering, but I had a strong party of Horse with me. I was (as I afterward found), in a disaffected house at the Head of Elk, but I was equally guarded agt friend and Foe."[74]

Washington's General Orders from his Quaker Hill headquarters on August 26 specified:

The officers commanding corps are to see that their men's arms are immediately cleaned and put in the best order possible; that the ammunition likewise be carefully inspected, and that the proper number of rounds for each man completed; that the bayonets fix well; that the flints be screwed in fast, and everything put in perfect readiness for action. The troops are without fail continually to have one day's provision of meat on hand, ready cooked and two days' ration of bread.[75]

For several days, Washington's Continentals had watched civilians—including women and children on foot driving cows or seated atop carts piled high with furniture—crowding the roads to Lancaster or Philadelphia. With sixteen thousand British and Hessian soldiers traveling up from Elkton and nearly eleven thousand Americans moving down Philadelphia Pike through Wilmington to Maryland Avenue and out toward the White Clay Creek, it seemed like the world was in motion.

On the twenty-eighth, General William Howe finally put his army in motion, forming his command into two columns across the Elk River. Captain Lieutenant Downman of the British artillery wrote, "A most fatiguing March, the roads exceeding bad, horses very bad, and the sun intensely hot, with nothing to eat or drink but apples and water."[76]

The left column was led by British general Cornwallis, who marched his men into Elkton. General William Howe took up his headquarters in the same Tory house where Washington had sought shelter two days before. He was pleased to find Elkton's "storehouses full, consisting of molasses, Indian corn, tobacco, pitch, tar and some cordage and flour" that the colonists had neglected to remove or destroy.

The British army camped beyond Elkton in quadrangle formation, and the Jägerkorps, with the light infantry and the Queen's Rangers, were posted in a wood in front of the army where two roads branch off to Christiana Bridge or Wilmington. On August 28, Captain Johann Ewald, a company commander in the Jägerkorps, a German troop with Howe's army, wrote:

> In this entire region we did not find a single living creature except wild animals; hence the army needed a guide, but the inhabitants had run off, taking with them all the livestock. Patrols were sent out on all sides to hunt for people and horses. But since this entire area was overgrown with woods, and we had no information about the enemy, no one was permitted to go any farther than where he could get support from the army.[77]

Despite Howe's best efforts—which included execution for marauders—his soldiers plundered without mercy. In some ways, the Americans were little better. Wilmington Friends records note:

> [T]he 28th of 8th month 1777, We are given to understand that friends meeting house in this town is taken up with soldiers who broke into it yesterday, and that although some friends demanding it to hold meeting in today, some of them promised we should have it by eleven o'clock, yet they

The Wilmington Monthly Meeting of the Religious Society of Friends has been located at Quaker Hill since 1738. The present meetinghouse, shown here, was built in 1817. John Dickinson is buried here. *David Ames, Center for Historic Architecture and Design, University of Delaware.*

did not perform, but kept possession and friends held meeting under a shady tree in the graveyard.[78]

In a chilling coincidence, on that exact same day in Philadelphia, the Continental Congress noted, "Quakers, render it certain and notorious, that those persons are, with much rancour and bitterness, disaffected to the American cause: that, as these persons will have it in their power, so there is no doubt it will be their inclination, to communicate intelligence to the enemy, and, in various other ways, to injure the councils and arms of America."[79]

The Continental Congress recommended that records of Quaker meetings be seized, called on the Pennsylvania Executive Council to arrest Quakers suspected of maintaining "a correspondence and connection highly prejudicial to the public safety" and urged every state to apprehend "all persons…who have, in their general conduct and conversation, evidenced a disposition inimical to the cause of America."

YANKEE DOODLE KEEP IT UP

The White Clay Creek joins Red Clay Creek about six miles southwest of Wilmington. Lieutenant James McMichael of the Pennsylvania Line wrote in his diary on August 28:

> *We marched from our encampment at 4 am and proceeding thro' Wilmington, Newport and Rising Sun (Stanton), encamped in the White Clay Creek Hundred, where we learned the enemy were near Newark and had driven in the Militia. Here we lay under arms, without tents, without blankets, as the waggons were left in the rear. A detachment of 150 men were sent out from Gen Weedon's brigade to observe the movements of the enemy. We expect a general attack tomorrow.*[80]

No sooner had Nathanael Greene's troops established camp at White Clay Creek than Washington, over Greene's objections, decided to withdraw two divisions to the east side of the Red Clay Creek, where the other divisions of the army would join them.[81]

On the twenty-ninth, George Washington wrote from his Wilmington headquarters to John Hancock:

> *The enemy advanced a part of their army yesterday to Gray's Hill about two miles on this side of Elk…Our light parties yesterday took between thirty and forty prisoners, twelve deserters from the navy and eight from the army have already come in, but they are able to give us very little intelligence. They generally agree that their troops are healthy but that their horse suffered very much by the voyage.*[82]

The same day, General Howe reported that the chasseurs encountered a body of the rebel infantry. A company commander in the British army's Hessian Field Jägerkorps, Johann Ewald, wrote, "On the 30th General Knyphausen crossed the Elk River to disperse an American Corps in the neighborhood, and to hunt up horses and slaughter cattle for the army. Toward evening the Jäger post was alarmed by the enemy, whereby a sentry was shot dead."[83]

In response, Washington's instructions to Brigadier General Caesar Rodney specifically stated:

Shellpot Mill, near Philadelphia Pike. *Delaware Public Archives.*

The more effectually to distress them in this respect, I would have you to remove such grain, cattle, horses, stock and other articles of subsistence, that lie so contiguous [to], and to continue doing this as they continue their progress through the country. You will also withdraw every kind of carriage which might serve to facilitate transportation of their baggage and stores to a distance from their Camp...them as to be in more immediate danger of falling into their hands.... One more precaution...if there should be any Mills in their neighborhood, to take away the runners and have them removed out of their reach—This will render the Mills useless to them, and will be little or no detriment to the Inhabitants, more especially the well affected, who it is probable will, for the most part, quit their homes, where they appear, and to whom they can be restored at a proper time...If the enemy should march toward Philadelphia, as is expected, you will hang constantly upon their right flank and rear, and give them all the annoyance in your power.[84]

HERE WE SAW THE MEN AND BOYS, AS THICK AS HASTY PUDDING

The impact on area residents can only be imagined. White Clay Creek miller Daniel Byrnes's nephew remembered:

> *A few days previous to the Battle of Brandywine, General Washington, with all his American army, were camped on rising ground before our door* [Red Clay Creek Mill near Stanton] *and round White Clay Creek Bridge farther westward; cannons were placed on this rise of ground for half a mile as thick as they could stand. General Washington's headquarters was at William Marshall's about the center of the army which is near the present meeting house in Stanton.*
>
> *The British army had landed below Elkton and was coming up the post road toward Christiana Bridge, and was hourly expected to appear in the front of the American army, about a mile and a half distant from them. Uncle Daniel's house and mill were right on the road about three quarters of a mile south of the American army. What a situation his and father's family were in. At this juncture, the battle was expected to commence every hour. The officers requested father to remove the family for they said the house would be shot down or torn to pieces with the cannon balls. Many families removed their goods some miles into the country.*
>
> *Uncle Daniel and our family remained, and I have heard my mother say that she intended when the battle began to take us children down into the cellar under the large arch which is under the chimney.*[85] *And in fact, their family was impacted, but not from the expected source. Wilmington Friends Meeting Book of Suffering noted, "Friends at White Clay Creek, the first being 9th month 1, 1777, Taken from Caleb Byrnes what was supposed to be six ton of hay by the American Army."*

On August 31, 1777, Ensign Carl Friedrich Rueffer of Hesse-Cassel von Mirbach Regiment wrote, "At every house we passed a pardon letter was nailed and a watch was posted to prevent looting."[86] But on that same day, Francis Alexander gave a deposition to Lieutenant Colonel George Latimer at the "Camp at Couches Mill" that "he was an Eye Witness to several Brutal ravages committed by the merciless Troops of the Tyrant of Great Britain on their late landing on the Head of Elk; that he particularly saw one of them, in the presence of divers others, ravish, or attempt violently to effect it, on the Person of a Young Woman of spotless Character living at his house, notwithstanding her cries and resistance to the contrary, at the same time making use of severe menaces in case of refusal; and sundry other acts of Barbarity he saw there perpetrated, shocking to humanity, and which cry aloud for vengeance."[87]

As the British and Hessians continued to advance, increasing numbers of local residents fled toward Lancaster. By the end of the week, even the Hessian soldiers were reporting incidents like this one:

> *Toward evening one of our patrols brought in a coach harnessed to six very fine horses. Found in the coach was Lady Patterson, the wife of an American Colonel—a lady who before autumn had overtaken her beauty must have been attractive—together with her maid, a dainty blonde, and three Negro servants. The entire baggage was thoroughly searched, and everything belonging to the Colonel was distributed among the jagers.... Since darkness fell over this partage d'Arlequin, and these ladies did not dare continue their journey at night, they were put up for the night in our gypsy dwelling, which were mostly nothing but huts of brushwood. At daybreak, after we had treated the ladies to breakfast and had exchanged their six good horses for six very patient ones, they resumed their journey. They bid us farewell and we wished them a pleasant journey. I do not believe they had ever dreamed in all their lives of making a toilette under such circumstances.*[88]

From Quaker Hill, Washington wrote to John Hancock and, later that day, to William Livingston:

> *How far the Enemy have it in view to extend themselves in a Line from Bay to Bay, I cannot determine; but the idea has taken pace with many... General How's Declaration is agreeable to his constant usage, and is what we might reasonably expect.... It is another Effort to seduce the people to give up their rights and to encourage our soldiery to desert.*[89]
>
> *You will ere this have heard of the enemy's advancing from the place of their first landing, and occupying with their van a piece of high ground called Gray's Hill.... All accounts agree that they are very much distressed for want of horses, numbers of which it is said died on the passage, and the rest are in exceedingly bad order, this will probably occasion some delay and give time for the militia, who seem to be collecting pretty fast to join us. We have light parties constantly hovering about them, who frequently make a few prisoners. The whole number already made is about seventy, and will be no inconsiderable check upon them.*[90]

Soldiers continued pouring into Delaware. Captain Robert Kirkwood, who grew up on Polly Drummond Road in northern New Castle County, wrote from the Pennsylvania State Headquarters, Chester, "Septr 1st. Tuesday. Sept 2nd Struck tents & march'd to Wilmington in the Delaware State & encamp'd about one Mile West of the town in all 13 miles."[91]

COOCH'S BRIDGE

The Philadelphia Campaign opened with the two armies clashing at the Battle of Cooch's Bridge about two and a half miles east of the Maryland border. On September 3, 1777, American brigadier general William Maxwell's corps of light infantry—composed of about eight hundred American riflemen from New Jersey, North Carolina, Pennsylvania, Virginia and Delaware militiamen—was hugely outnumbered but bravely fought well-trained Hessian and Ansbach Jägers and British light infantrymen.

Cooch's Bridge. Photographed by Bob Barnes. *Postcard from the Pencader Heritage Collection.*

VOICES OF THE PAST

The eyewitness account of Lieutenant Heinrich Carl Philipp von Feilitsch of the Ansbach-Bayreuth Jägers, follows:

> *The 3rd—We marched out of our camp at four o'clock in the morning… thereafter encountered an enemy corps of 3,000 men in the region of… Katschers Mill (Cooch's Mill). The enemy stood firm. The fire was extremely heavy and lasted about two hours. Only our corps [i.e., the jägers] was engaged and a few English. The enemy attacked three times. We lost one dead and ten wounded, while the rebels suffered nearly fifty dead and, according to the deserters, very many wounded. We made few prisoners. Our jaegers conducted themselves well and, after the enemy was driven back, we entered camp during the afternoon not far from that place. The affair began at eight o'clock and lasted until ten. The company had two wounded, a corporal and a jaeger.[92]*

A British account reported:

> [A]*dvanced about seven miles, on the road towards Christeen Bridge. At the entrance of a wood, five miles from town, the rebels began to fire upon the advanced corps of Rangers and Chassears; and a smart skermesh continued for some time; till a few shots from one of our field pieces drove the rebels entirely off. The first battalion of light infantry endeavoured to turn their left flank, and just when they thought it was completed unluckily met with an unpassable swamp, and were obliged to return by the way they went.… The rebels in this affair had upwards of thirty men killed. Our loss was trifling.… A little in front is Goughs Mill and bridge, over a part of Christeen creek—the light infantry was posted beyond the bridge, and our line extended thence backwards, to one Aikens house, the present headquarters, between four and five miles from Elk, and there we halted a few days.[93]*

That evening, George Washington summed up the day's events:

From Headquarters: Wilmington, Del
September 3, 1777. 8 o Clock P.M.

Sir:

...This Morning the Enemy came out with considerable force and three pieces of Artillery, against our Light Advanced Corps, and after some pretty smart skirmishing obliged them to retreat, being far inferior in number and without Cannon. The loss on either side is not yet ascertained. Ours, tho' not exactly known, is not very considerable. Theirs, we have reason to believe, was much greater, as some of our parties, composed of expert Marksmen, had Opportunities of giving them several close, well-directed fires; more particularly in One instance, when a body of Riflemen formed a kind of Ambuscade. They advanced about Two miles this side of Iron Hill, and then withdrew to that place, leaving a picket at Coach's Mill [sic], about a mile in Front. Our parties now lie at White Clay Creek, except the advanced pickets which are at Christiana Bridge.... The design of their movement this morning seems to have been to disperse our Light Troops, who had been troublesome to them, and to gain possession of Iron Hill to establish a post most probably for covering their retreat in case of accidents.

I have the Honor to be with great respect Sir, Yr Most Obedt servt.
Geo Washington[94]

As the sounds of the Battle of Cooch's Bridge echoed across the fields, a rider from Philadelphia brought the Friends at White Clay Creek a frightening message. The day before, by the order of the Pennsylvania Supreme Executive Council and by recommendation of the Continental Congress, twenty well-respected Philadelphia Quakers had been imprisoned without a hearing. The Society of Friends' deliberately neutral position on the war had triggered the fears of the Continental Congress that Quakers were "enemies of their country" and that if the British did indeed capture Philadelphia, area residents would continue to follow the pacifist examples of these longtime social and business leaders.

In the days that followed, the British raided Christiana. Captain William Dansey wrote exuberantly to his mother in Brinsop, Herefordshire, that a "flanking party" of his 33rd Regiment of Foot "took the horse, arms, colors, and drums belonging to a rebel Colonel of the Delaware Militia. Made his brother prisoner and caused all his Baggage to be taken, which the General very politely sent back again. But the horse, arms, colors came to my share."[95]

The September 5, 1777 *Pennsylvania Evening Post* posted the remonstrance of the Quaker prisoners Israel Pemberton, John Hunt and Samuel Pleasants, claiming the rights of freemen against arbitrary confinement. On September 6, Congress approved a recommendation that records seized from the confined Quakers should be published.

For the next five days, Cornwallis used the Cooch home as his headquarters. Two days after the battle, his aide, Major John André, drew a map showing British units posted around the Cooch house. According to family legend, the officers drank all of Cooch's liquor, and the troops burned Cooch's gristmill when they left.

Maxwell's Corps and the Delaware militia returned to the main Continental lines near Stanton. That morning, September 6, 1777, Quaker pacifist Daniel Byrnes, with a wife and several children still at home, received word that his house would be the site of a Council of War. That very evening, Generals Greene, Lafayette, Maxwell, Sullivan and Wayne were among those in attendance.[96]

The General Orders for the day can be found in both the papers of George Washington and Robert Kirkwood's journal:

> *The General begs the favor of the officers to be attentive to all strange faces and suspicious characters which may be discovered in camp; and upon examination of them no good account can be given why they are there, to carry them to the Major General of the day for further examination; this, as it is only a necessary precaution, is to be done in a manner least offensive. The General Officers are to meet at 5 O'Clock this afternoon at the brick house by White-Clay creek, and fix upon proper picquets for the security of the camp. John Laurens and Peter Presley Thornton Esqrs. are appointed Extra-Aids-Du-Camp to the Commander in Chief: all orders therefore thro' them in writing, or otherwise, are to be regarded in the same light as if proceeding from any other of his Aide-du-Camp.*[97]

Many years later, their inadvertent host, Daniel Byrnes, wrote to George Washington presenting his side of the story:

> *In the year 1777 I was owner of and Lived at them Mills in the State of Dallaware on the side of White Clay Creek abought two Miles north of Christiana Bridge at the time the English Army Lay between my Mills*

Hale Byrnes House, near Stanton, Delaware. *Delaware Public Archives.*

and the head of Elk and the American Army Some of them on the Hill by White Clay Creek Bridge in Sight of my House & Mills and Some of them nearer to Newport. Thus was I with my Famely Situated between the two Contending Armies and on the 7ᵗʰ Day of the week Clement Biddle,[98] *an officer as I Supose in thy Army Came to my House and informed me that General Woshington had Sent him to let me know that the wheat & Flour in my Mills must be Removed and told me that thou Said the English Army wod be quite likely to Come that way and wod Distroy what I had but that thou wod take it and I Should be paid for it. I Did then belive thou intended it as a favour to me as I was not Looked on as an Enemy to my Countery and therefore I could Do no other thing but Submit to thy orders accordingly he Sent that Day twenty Wagons and Loaded with Wheat and Flour and next Day being first Day of the week came twenty more Wagons and Loaded (while I was at Meeting) with wheat and flour they also that*

Day took Eight Large Cheese away which was put in the Mill to be out of the way of the Flies they Laft with Some of my young men Recipts for the Wheat & Flour but not for the Cheese they ware to come again the Next Day being the Second Day of the week for more wheat & Flour as there was Some Still Lafft but that Day the English Army Crossed white Clay Creek 2 or 3 miles above my Mills and thy Army moved away. I saw Clement Biddle that Day on Horseback he told me he wod pay me but the Army was moving and all Seemed in a hurry. I Supose he had not time and want away without paying after that time there was Much Difficulties with the Army I knew not whare to apply for pay.[99]

A Steep Defile

At four o'clock in the morning on September 8, 1777, the British 1st Division under General Cornwallis, accompanied by General Howe, started to march. Then the 2nd Division under General Grant followed and then the 3rd Division under General von Knyphausen,

which had with it all our baggage, a lot of cattle, provisions, and other wagons. All marched in one column, and to our great surprise, instead of taking the road by way of Christians Bridge to Wilmington as expected, we went to our left by way of White Clay Creek and Newark. We halted near Nicolson's, the only house on the main road from Newport and Wilmington to Lancaster. Knyphausen's rear guard did not arrive until two o'clock in the morning. Everyone is pleased with the good march and the fact that it was kept a secret, thus cutting off Washington from Lancaster.[100]

Several British officers remarked about seeing an aurora borealis in the sky as they left their Glasgow-area camps: "8th. The whole moved 2 hours before daylight—a remarkable borealis. An amazing; strong ground—marched this day about 12 miles to Head Quarters—a very strong country—but 3 or 4 Shots fired during the march. A great deal of rebel cattle collected."[101]

The soldiers' descriptions of Newark give us a clear picture of what they saw. James Parker observed:

The country is entirely deserted. We pass the Village of Newark, remarkable for Sedition and Presbetarian sermons, the inhabitants have all left their houses.[102]

Richardson House, near Maryland Avenue, Newport, Delaware. *Delaware Public Archives.*

Ensign Carl Friedrich Rueffer of Hesse-Cassel von Mirbach related:

> *At two o'clock we passed Newark, a very pleasantly built town of about sixty houses, but completely uninhabited. Also, now and again, very pleasing country homes which previous to this time we had seldom encountered in this area because it is rather thinly settled.*[103]

As they climbed the hill past Newark to White Clay Creek, the ground grew steeper and rougher. Today, area historians argue about the precise location of the "steep defile" mentioned by commander of the Hessian Jäger corps, Johann Ewald, but the ground between Newark and Lancaster Pike, especially near Pike Creek, remains a hair-raising land formation:

> *The army marched past Newark and toward morning on the 8th crossed the White Clay Creek, which was surrounded on both sides by steep, rocky heights that formed a most frightful defile half an hour in length. I still cannot understand why Sullivan abandoned this position, where a hundred riflemen could have held up the army a whole day and killed many men. My hair stood on end as we crammed into the defile, and I imagined nothing*

more certain than an unexpected attack at the moment when we would have barely stuck our nose out of the defile. For the precipitous rocks on both sides of the creek and along the defile were so steep that no one could scale them. But I surmised Sullivan had reasoned that General Howe would never choose this route, because he had stationed himself behind the Christiana Bridge. He had interspersed the marshy bank with thirty cannon, making a good defile there, which position was now bypassed during this march.[104]

British general James Grant took an alternative road to Chadds Ford and marched at sunset "by a bye road to Hokerson Meeting House—Quaker meeting 4 miles' distance" and encamped along Old Wilmington Road for the night.

As the Americans got wind that the British were packing up and moving northward, they began to do the same. Captain Joseph Clark of the 3rd Virginia wrote:

Our situation near Newport was such that the enemy could not pass that way to Philadelphia without meeting our army, and thereby bringing on a general engagement, they, this night (Monday night) by a by-road, with good guides, got privately round our right wing of encampment and was advancing towards Philadelphia by the Lancaster Road. We, however, got word of it in time, and the whole army moved at 1 or 2 o'clock at night.[105]

On September 9, 1777, Samuel Chase, a Maryland delegate to the Continental Congress, wrote to Maryland's Governor Thomas Johnson about the action in Delaware:

I have no letter from you by yesterday's Post. Mr. Lux informs me that you have regular and quick Intelligence from Head Quarters. We are in daily expectation of a Battle. Howe's whole army are on this side of Iron Hill, in three Divisions. Howes head-quarters are at Aitkens tavern, Cornwallis at Coaches Mill, and Kniphausen near Christiana Bridge…If the fleet is gone down our Bay, I think Annapolis and Baltimore will be safe this Year.
My compliments to the Gentlemen of the Council.

Your Affectionate and obedient Servt.
Saml Chase

P.S. An officer just from Camp informs the Enemy are advancing[106]

On the same day, George Washington sent a message to John Hancock in Philadelphia recounting the past two days' adventures:

8 Miles from Wilmington [Delaware] *9ᵗʰ Sept. 1777*

Sir:

The Enemy advanced yesterday with a seeming intention of attacking us upon our post near Newport. We waited for them the whole day, but they halted in the Evening at a place called Mill Town about two Miles from us. Upon reconnoitering their Situation, it appeared probable that they only meant to amuse us in front, while their real intent was to march by our Right and by suddenly passing the Brandywine and gaining the heights upon the North side of that River, get between us and Philada and cut us off from that City. To prevent this, it was judged expedient to change our position immediately, the Army accordingly marched at two O'clock this morning and will take post this Evening upon the High Grounds near Chad's Ford. We have heard nothing circumstantial from the Enemy this day. When I do, I shall immediately transmit you an Account.

I have the Honor to be Sir, Yr most obt Servt,
Go: Washington.[107]

SEPTEMBER 11, 1777, AND AFTERMATH

On the day of the Battle of Brandywine, the Delaware Continental Regiment was assigned to defend Painter's Ford, north of Chadds Ford and ferry. Robert Kirkwood noted in his journal, "[O]ur Regt was Sent as A flanking party on the Enemy's left wing, during the engagement we were Several times exposed to the fire of the enemy's Cannon and Small arms. About sunset retreated to Chester, being 15 miles."[108] At midnight, Washington wrote to John Hancock from Chester, "I am sorry to inform you that in this day's engagement we have been obliged to leave the enemy masters of the field…we have also lost seven or eight pieces of cannon, according to the best information I can at present obtain."[109]

A cannon shot can be heard for forty miles. Residents of Wilmington could hear the battle and tracked the day's events by sending young boys up Concord Pike to see what was going on. An eyewitness later recounted, "During the progress of the Battle of Brandywine many of us saw from the top of the house, formerly John Dickenson's, in Market Street, the smoke of the engagement and heard the reports of the cannon and the rattle of the platoon firing of that bloody day."[110]

Following the Battle of the Brandywine, British general Howe dispatched the 71st Regiment, Frazer's Highlanders, to Wilmington, Delaware. Except for one of the three regular battalions and the flank companies, this large unit of about one thousand men had been kept in reserve during the battle, assigned to guard the baggage. Howe's purpose in seizing Wilmington was to create a point of rendezvous with Admiral Howe and the British fleet.

It is said that the invaders were annoyed by a sign before Marshall's Hotel on the corner of Third and Market Streets showing the American sloop-of-war *Randolph* victorious over a British vessel. Two sailors brought axes with which they chopped down the pole, splitting the sign into tiny bits.[111]

A British officer's journal noted, "This day the 71st Regt. took possession of Wilmington, the rebels having left 7 pieces of Cannon unspiked and also 2 Brass field pieces taken from the Hessians at Trenton."[112] A Hessian diary noted that "Governor McKinley of Delaware, who was late in leaving the city, was captured by the Scots."[113]

On September 13, American colonel Mordecai Gist reported from Christiana:

> [T]*he sick and Wounded of the Enemy came into Wilmington yesterday with the prisoners they took in the late Engagement. They brought with them five pieces of Artillery and have a Guard of Near 1,000 men, chiefly Highlanders and Hessians, who are busily employed in fortifying the Heights, particularly around the Academy. I dispatched a party last Night to Surprise and bring off their Picket Guard, but through the Misconduct of the Guide, failed in the attempt. Our party drove them in to their Main Body and returned with a man Wounded. Colonel Rodney's Men having all deserted him to about 75, he left me at this place in the Evening of the 13*[th] *Inst. I shall send an Express to him with your orders.*[114]

A British accounts noted, "The sick and wounded were escorted to Willmington [*sic*] (a few miles below Chester); near which we have squadron of men of war; and the general hospital is established there."[115] Hessian records show the activity of their troops under the command of Colonel Johann von Loos:

"Perspective View of the Country between Wilmington and the Delaware. Taken from the Hill S.W. of the Academy." Published in the *Columbian Magazine, or Monthly Miscellany* for April 1787. Philadelphia, printed for Seddon, Spotswood, Cist and Trenchard. *Society of Cincinnati.*

We started at 6 o'clock on the morning of the 14th and escorted the wounded belonging to our army and 350 prisoners to Wilmington, a beautiful little town surrounded by two rivers, the Brandywine and the Christine, both of which flow into the Delaware close to this place.

On the March thither we destroyed a magazine belonging to the rebels containing arms, cartridge pouches, and clothing. Colonel MacDonald with 3 Battalions Scotch Highlanders had already taken possession of Wilmington; the small rebel garrison had been surprised by him in the night. In a fort in the direction of the Delaware, we found 7 guns. All the troops which were now under command of Colonel von Loos encamped on a height before the town, and fortified themselves as well as circumstances permitted, as we had not much Artillery with us.[116]

The main bodies of the occupying troops were stationed toward the center of town, where they built a fort and two palisades extending north and south on the west side of town and along part of the King's Road to Baltimore. They also built a camp of huts sunk two or three feet into the ground on West Street extending from Delaware Avenue to the top of the hill above the Brandywine River. At the bridge over the Brandywine, they built a redoubt, manned by a captain, a subaltern and one hundred men. An officer and twenty-nine chasseurs were posted on the Brandywine near today's Broome Street.[117]

Among the most interesting insights into the occupation of Wilmington is a series of published oral history interviews triggered by the excitement surrounding Lafayette's triumphant return in 1824–25:

> *They* [American prisoners of the British] *were all placed under the horse shed at Lawson's tavern, now belonging to James Canby, where they remained about 60 hours and then were removed across the street to the Presbyterian Meeting House. John Ferriss proposed to two others to go up and see our townsmen thus imprisoned, and furnish them with some eatables or inquire of them, for it was said they had been hardly dealt with. As we approached the tavern we saw them marched across the street and through the northwest gate, and they placed themselves on the southeast side of the interior, which prevented our speaking to any of them. The officer in command on the street-side of the board fence was on the left of the gate and we three were on the other side of the gate, on the street side also, the open gate between us, which was soon shut. The sentinel had rested his gun with fixed bayonets against the wall of the house; the officer imperiously directed him to take his gun and work clear of the wall and the fence, so as to be able to use it freely—for these, said he (using harsh language), might attempt to make their escape.*
>
> *J.F. observed they were all respectable persons and would not attempt it (or words to that effect.) This irritated the officer and he then turned his harsh language on us, and concluded in saying they had "no friends in this country but Quakers" (in which idea he was far wrong), and that "he doubted not but we deserved to be there, imprisoned as those." The word Quaker I took up, and observed to him mildly that we were Quakers. He excused himself and invited us to his rooms in the tavern, to take a glass of wine, which we did and saved ourselves from further insult.*[118]

> *When the British troops took possession of Wilmington, in 1777, I was a boy of about 14 years of age, and though somewhat alarmed, at first, by new faces and the broad Scotch and Hessian Dutch languages, also new to me, yet a few weeks rendered me very familiar with many of the officers and soldiers of both these nations—and being of playful disposition, I became a favorite with several wounded officers, young men, who were billeted in the house adjoining that in which I lived.*[119]

> *The wounded soldiers in the house now occupied by John Rumford, cruelly tied a pistol barrel, charged alternatively with wet and dry powder, to a*

Old First Presbyterian Church, South Park Drive at West Street, moved from Tenth and Market, Wilmington. *HABS-HAER, Library of Congress.*

dog's tail, and having set it on fire opposite their door directed the dog down the street, the first discharge took place nearly opposite the hotel now kept by John M. Smith; the second somewhat lower down the street—and the third and last, opposite the Doctors' Quarters. These different reports being similar to the regular alarm of sentinel firing, created great agitation, as though an attack had commenced; but it soon subsided, when it was discovered that it arose from the fun of soldiers, who, though suffering from their own wounds, felt a pleasure in inflicting pain upon the "rebel dog."[120]

Curiously enough, that rabid Patriot Thomas McKean strongly believed that the Quakers arrested earlier in September had the right to habeas corpus and should not be detained as prisoners without a hearing. On Sunday, September 14, a bill was passed in Philadelphia that removed the issue from McKean's jurisdiction. The suspension of habeas corpus, in the opinion of Tories and conservatives, was "the very extreme of tyranny" but was deemed necessary by the Continental Congress. The council was

Thomas McKean (1734–1817). *Delaware Public Archives.*

anxious "that some account of this transaction should be given to the public as these people mean to publish and raise a ferment."[121]

On September 15, 1777, the winds shifted to the northeast and increased in violence. The sky grew overcast and ominous, and the clouds became dark and heavy with moisture. The weather seemed appropriate. Wilmington Friends received word on the eighteenth that Jehu Hollingsworth, a member of its own monthly meeting, had been imprisoned in a Lancaster jail for refusing to comply with the "Test Act," a new policy that demanded he, as a stranger, swear allegiance to Pennsylvania. The minutes of the meeting also noted that Daniel Byrnes and the Friends at White Clay Creek were absent from the meeting, "by reason, we suppose, of the difficulty of passing and repassing, any friend who may have opportunity are desired to notify them of the time." On September 25, 1777, eleven Wilmington Quakers met as planned, noting that Daniel Byrnes was not in attendance. They approved a letter of support written to Jehu Hollingsworth and agreed to sign it and forward it "by the first convenient opportunity."[122]

Announcing their Quaker prisoners would be sent to Staunton, Virginia, members of Continental Congress fled Philadelphia, resolving to meet wherever and whenever it safely could. At Paoli on the night of September 20, the British launched a vicious attack on General Anthony Wayne's camp, bayoneting more than three hundred men. The British forces now had the command of Wilmington and New Castle and controlled the entire western shoreline of the Delaware River and Bay. British general Howe entered Philadelphia on September 26.

On that day, Thomas McKean wrote to George Read, who had taken his family to New Jersey, explaining that because of the captivity of President McKinly and Read's absence in Philadelphia, he felt it his duty to take emergency measures in Delaware to protect "the virtuous part of the people." McKean urged Read to return home as quickly as possible, and in his capacity as acting president, McKean appointed Caesar Rodney major general of the militia and John Dagworthy and Samuel Patterson as brigadiers. Caesar Rodney wrote, "[We] had no more of the Delaware Militia than Sufficient to Conduct their baggage home; am sorry to say, to no purpose [I have] been trying to rouse and Get them to the field again."[123]

During the British occupation of Wilmington, the Delaware Continental Regiment was nearby but not in the new state. It had been busy at Paoli and then, on October 4, 1777, was part of the surprise attack on the British camp at Germantown, Pennsylvania, where foggy weather and confusion had forced another American retreat. On the fifth, Captain Peery in Lewes informed Caesar Rodney that "36 sail of the enemy ships went past this town up the Bay, and this evening 47 more were seen from the Light house standing in for the Cape, they have anchored in our road." Rodney sent Samuel Patterson to St. Georges, Delaware, to rally the militia, but Patterson had little luck. "There is not a field officer here," Patterson wrote, "no hopes of getting them to Guard their Shore as long as the Enemy lay there…I don't much blame them, as all our big men have left us. I wish sincerely you would come, if only with your [light] horse, to give some heart. If no help, the few I have will disperse."[124]

Because the presence of the British fleet in the Delaware River, McKean established a temporary capital of the state farther inland, at Newark, and agreeing with Patterson's assessment, he wrote to George Washington on October 8 that the people were "dispirited and dispersed." He continued, "The Tories & less virtuous part that remained" were daily employed in supplying the British troops, both in Wilmington and at Newcastle on board the ships of war, with all kinds of provisions.[125]

By mid-October, the British fleet was anchored in the Delaware River all the way from New Castle to Port Penn. The British army, slightly swelled by additions from the Delaware Loyalists, would soon relocate to Philadelphia, now in British hands. On October 12, Ambrose Serle, British secretary to Lord Howe, described his trip upstream to Wilmington:

> *Sailed up the creek to Wilmington. The town is scattered in its buildings, and situated upon the side of an eminence, which commands a fine prospect of the Delaware and the opposite shore of New Jersey. There are two places for markets, but no buildings public or private of much account. It is certainly in a good situation for trade, and inhabited principally by Quakers, who though decent and passive, have not escaped distress from the hands of the rebels. I had some conversation with an intelligent elderly*

George Read (1733–1798). *Delaware Public Archives.*

man, who informed me of the great necessities of the country for most of the comforts and conveniencies of life. They feel very deeply the horrors of this unnatural war, which the wickedness and wantoness of some of their principal people have brought upon them.[126]

On October 1, 1777, George Read finally arrived to take over the reins of the state government. In Salem, New Jersey, he was finally able to get a boat to take his family the five miles across the river. Their boat had almost reached the Delaware shore when British men-of-war lying at anchor off New Castle dispatched an armed barge in pursuit of her. At low tide, their boat grounded so far from the beach that it was impossible for Mr. Read and his family to land before their pursuers reached them. Read politely represented himself to them simply as a country gentleman who, with his wife and infant children, was returning home from New Jersey. The British accordingly helped land the baggage and assisted him in bringing the ladies and children to shore."[127]

Two weeks later, the British and Hessian forces began evacuating Wilmington. Years later, a resident interviewed in the *American Watchman* remembered a childhood scene:

> *The boys of the town had a charming employment in plundering the deserted camp where we found a great variety of articles that were a treasure to us—particularly powder and ball, etc., they served us for amusement for a long time afterwards. The writer has particular cause to remember some of these circumstances from a severe burn that he received on one of the occasions when we used to "flash" whole cartridges of powder—so plenty with us was this precious but mischievous article.[128]*

DAMNING THE WHIGS

Now that the British had captured Philadelphia, hundreds of Delaware Tories flocked to Lewes, "drinking the health of King George, damning the Whigs, and daring the rebels to arrest them." When the Whigs tried to enforce the taking of an oath of allegiance as a test for voting, the enraged Tories threatened to throw them "Neck and Heels out of the Courthouse." After Major Henry Fisher threatened to make Lewes "too hot for every Loyalist in it," Isaac Bradley and others assaulted him with fists, clubs and feet. It is said that someone fired a gun at Bradley; the militia had to rescue Henry Fisher, and the Tories fled through the windows of the courthouse pursued by Patriot soldiers.

The British, needing clear access up the river to supply their winter encampment in Philadelphia, had worked diligently to clear the river of Patriot-made obstructions. The warships *Augusta, Roebuck, Liverpool, Pearl* and *Merlin* passed through an opening in the lower line of chevaux-de-frises and moved up the river with the flowing tide. But the artificial obstructions had

Explosion of the Augusta. Photographed by Tyler Rudd Putman. From Justin Winsor's *Narrative and Critical History of America*, vol. 6 (Houghton, Mifflin and Company, 1887).

altered the course of the channel and raised sandbanks where none existed before. As the tide fell, both the *Augusta* and the *Merlin* went aground a little below the second row of chevaux-de-frises. At the return of the tide, the *Roebuck*'s attempt to free them was in vain. A sporadic exchange of cannon fire lasted nearly three hours.

According to an American eyewitness, at about 2:00 p.m. the *Augusta* caught fire near its stern. The fire spread rapidly; soon the entire vessel was wrapped in flames, and the ship exploded.[129] The blast smashed windows in Philadelphia and was heard up to thirty miles away and remarked on in both Germantown, Pennsylvania, and Wilmington, Delaware. The loss of the ship was attributed to various causes. John Montresor, British officer in charge of the Siege of Fort Mifflin, wrote that one lieutenant, the ship's chaplain and sixty other men were killed while struggling in the water. Soon after, the crew of the *Merlin* abandoned ship and set their ship on fire to keep it out of American hands. The *Merlin* blew up later that day. The reports of the cannons were usually heard when the wind was favorable. But on that day, the wind was very strong from the northwest, and nothing was heard until the afternoon, when the bottles and other glassware in Dr. Way's shop on Market Street, Wilmington, were rattling from the explosion.[130]

Map of Wilmington, Delaware, by Friedrich Adam Julius von Wangenheim, 1777. Scale about 1:38,000. Pen-and-ink and pencil on tracing paper. Oriented with north toward the upper right. Relief shown by hachures. Title in French. *Library of Congress.*

On December 19, 1777, Maryland troops of Sullivan's Division were detached and sent along with Hazen's Regiment to occupy Wilmington, while the bulk of the army went on to Valley Forge. About 1,500 soldiers, under the command of Maryland's General Smallwood, settled in near what is now Lovering and Broom Streets. Quaker records state, "A division of the American Army wintered here and Friends were much oppressed having both officers and soldiers placed in their families."

1778

The garrison, composed largely of Delaware and Maryland soldiers under Smallwood's command, served as a buffer between the American supply depots at Head of Elk and the British in Philadelphia, as an intelligence station for monitoring river traffic and as a support base for Continental forays into New Jersey. By the middle of March 1778, the soldiers in Wilmington were equally as hungry as their colleagues at Valley Forge. Reduced to scavenging Delaware for food, Smallwood complained that the area was "intirely drained." The men confined their efforts to watching the river for enemy shipping, removing hay from its banks between Wilmington and Chester and retrieving the cargoes of several British vessels captured in the area. At Congress's request, Smallwood detached a party of men to arrest citizens of questionable political allegiance in anticipation of a British invasion of Delaware.

Chapter 9

WILMINGTON IN THE WINTER
OF VALLEY FORGE

At Valley Forge, American quartermaster Major Nathanael Greene protested. Hundreds of horses had starved to death, and the men were ragged and hungry. He led foraging expeditions far and wide in search of food and supplies. On February 15, 1778, Nathanael Greene came to Delaware. Here, he wrote, "The residents cry out and beset me from all quarters, but like Pharaoh, I harden my heart." Finding two men along the road bringing provisions intended for the civilian market, he "gave them a hundred lashes each by way of example."[131]

A major coup took place around that same time when two barges rowed past Philadelphia in the dark. At dawn, John Barry sought out General Smallwood. A week later, four Pennsylvania navy barges and three hundred soldiers from Valley Forge commanded by Brigadier General Anthony Wayne joined them. On February 19, the barges crossed to New Jersey for cattle. Wayne's men moved several hundred head of cattle north, crossing the river above Philadelphia, while Barry, as a diversionary tactic, took the barges south, stopping to burn every haystack he could find in the hopes of drawing the British forces away from Wayne. Their deception worked. Washington happily received the cattle at Valley Forge, while Captain Andrew Snape Hammond of the *Roebuck* sent several boatloads of redcoats across the Delaware to catch the hay burners. After the second day of this bluff, Barry's men narrowly escaped to the small fishing village of Port Penn, near Reedy Point.[132]

Washington and Lafayette at Valley Forge. *Special Collections, Skillman Library, Lafayette College.*

PORT PENN

Ice covered the Delaware River for a week but had thawed by March 7. A letter from Port Penn brought Washington some exciting news:

To George Washington from Captain John Barry, 9 March 1778
Port Penn [Delaware River] *March 9th 1778*

Dear General
Tis with the Greatest Satisfaction Imaginable I inform You of Capturing Two Ships & a Schooner of the Enemy. The two ships were Transports from Rhode Island Loaded with forage One Mounting Six Four Pounders with fourteen hands Each the Schooner is in the Engineering Department Mounting Eight Double fortified four Pounders & twelve four Pound howitz Properly fitted in Every Particular & Manned with thirty-three men.
Among the Prisoners is a Lieutenant in the Same Department with the Schooner the Lieutenant together with the Captain of the Schooner Being Verry Solicitous for the Liberty of a Fortnight thought Proper by the Advice

of Nicholas Vandyke Esqr. [a Member of Congress] *to allow them their Parole for a fortnight to Go to Philadelphia with Some Officers Lady's that were taken in the Schooner, the Schooner is a most Excellent Vessel for Our Purpose & as there Are a Number of Ships Expected in Under Verry Little Convoy with the farther assistance of about forty men should Give a Verry Good account of them, as the Enemy are Greatly Necessitated for want of Forage, the Schooner is Unloaded But have not as Yet the Manifest of the Cargo But are a Number of Engineering Tools on Board.*

Shall Give You a Circumstantial account of the Whole Cargo as Soon as Possible. By the Bearer Mr John Chilton have Sent You a Cheese Together with a Jar of Pickled Oysters which Crave Your Acceptance should have Remitted the Particulars Together with the Letters & Dispatch for General De hester Before But a fleet of the Enemys Small Vessels appearing in Sight Obliged me to Burn One of the Ships & am afraid the Other will share the same fate after Discharging her But am Determined to hold the Schooner at all Events Inclosed You have the Articles of the Schooners Capitulation as we Sent a flag on Board her After Boarding the two Ships & am Sir with Due Respect Your Excellncies Most Obedient Humbl. Servt

John Barry[133]

Brigadier General William Smallwood followed up from Wilmington on March 9 with his own letter to Washington at Valley Forge:

Capt. Barry applied on Saturday Night about 12 Oclock for a Detachment to aid & support him in securing & unlading two Ships & a Schooner which he had taken that afternoon, about Reedy Island, in conjunction with some Armed Boats of this Neighbourhood, one of the Ships mounts 6 and the Schooner 8 carriage Guns, he cou'd not inform what their Loadings were, I advised bringing them up this Creek, but have not heard from him since, but have understood he has hauled them in the Piers at Pt Penn, & that the upper part of their holds, are stowed with Hay.

In much haste remain your Excellency's very Obedt Hble Sert
W. Smallwood

Wilmington March 10ᵗʰ 1778 Since I wrote the above an Officer from Capt. Barry came last Night with a Bag of L[ette]rs &c. on his way to address them to you who will inform you more particularly of this Affair...

Our People were attacked at 2 OClk off Pt Pen by a 20 Gun Ship & an Armed Sloop which it was supposed were convoying the Remainder of the Forage Fleet—I have received Intelligence that many of the Enemy are out of Philada above their Lines towards German Town but the Intelligence is not to be depended on.

I am as above &c.
W.S.

N.B. one of the Lieutenants gives an Account of 100 Transports being ordered round to Delaware abt the middle of this Month &c[134]

TREATY OF AMITY AND COMMERCE

The single most important diplomatic success of the colonists during the War of Independence was the critical link forged with France that winter. On February 6, 1778, Benjamin Franklin, Arthur Lee and Silas Deane had signed a Treaty of Alliance and a Treaty of Amity and Commerce with France. Startled by the American victory at Saratoga the previous October and fearful of the consequences of the French and American alliance, British prime minister Lord North convinced Parliament to establish a commission headed by Frederick Howard, the Fifth Earl of Carlisle, to negotiate a settlement with the Continental Congress. The commissioners set sail for America. When Parliament offered the colonies a return to the antebellum status quo on March 16, 1778—that is, they offered to grant all American demands short of independence—it was too late. By that time, the American Congress, and most of the American people, had decided that self-determination was the best course.

Andrew Snape Hamond of the *Roebuck* tried to protect the shipping in the Delaware River and Bay for the supplies needed by the British quartered in Philadelphia. On March 10, he ordered the *Pearl* to station itself between Chester and Reedy Point and to destroy all rebel-armed boats found in the mouths of the creeks in the Wilmington area. Protection was to be offered to all boats bringing produce to Philadelphia markets. Two days later, Captain Phipps, with the *Camilla*, was ordered to proceed down the river and patrol the area between Reedy Island and Bombay Hook. After five days, they reached Reedy Point opposite Salem Creek. The boats of the British men-

MAL LUI VEUT MAL LUI TOURNE DIT LE BON HOMME RICHARD

Sujet Mémorable des Révolutions de l'Univers

French political cartoon dated 1778 showing a man with feathered cap labeled "Ameriquain" (representing America) cutting the horns off a cow labeled "Commerce d'Angleterre" (British commerce); two men labeled "Francois" and "Espagnol" (France and Spain) are standing toward the rear of the cow holding bowls of milk. *Library of Congress.*

of-war *Pearl* and *Camilla* took the rebel boat *Fame* out of a creek just above Reedy Point.

A few miles south of Port Penn, the British raided Delaware farms and traded with Tories for supplies at Liston's Point and Thoroughfare Neck. George Read reported that "a considerable body of the Enemy supposed to be 700 landed this morning about Listen's Highlands and were on the march up the Thoroughfare Neck." Charles Pope, commander of Delaware's Continental Regiment, corrected this information, writing to Caesar Rodney from Duck Creek that "30 or 40 marines landed & took off some cattle etc., & returned…at eight o'clock this morning. The fleet consisting of about 35 sail weighed and stood Down the Bay."[135] In Lewes, it was reported on March 24 that a "fleet of 40 Sail" was seen going up the bay the previous night.

Reedy Point, near Port Penn, Delaware. *Guy Harrington.*

Because New Castle was dangerously close to the river, the Delaware Assembly once again met in Dover. In a vote of twenty to four, Caesar Rodney was elected president of Delaware for a term of three years.

Chapter 10

REFUGEES AND TORIES

In the meantime, former Delaware president John McKinly was still a British prisoner in Philadelphia. Thomas McKean angrily wrote to George Read, "I was told the other day that he lodged at widow Jenkins's along with his old friends Robinson and Manlove and he seemed very happy." Rodney refused to condemn McKinly on such flimsy evidence and told him that he was "well informed that Robinson has lodged at Joshua Fisher's ever since he went to the City and that Manlove's place of Abode is at one Snowden's over the Drawbridge."[136]

News from Lewes included the following notes: "English burn the 2 last vessels ashore, ye woods burn. John Whiltbanck, Loyalist, Went with Negroes to ye English." As the weather grew warmer, Caesar Rodney noted from Dover in the spring of 1778, "We are constantly alarmed in this place by the enemy and refugees. And seldom has a day passed but some man in this and the neighbouring counties is taken off by the villains. So that men near the Bay who I know to be hearty in the Cause, dare neither act nor speak lest they should be taken away and their houses plundered."[137]

Joshua Hill, prominent landowner and member of the Delaware Assembly, spoke harshly about Congress and the measures taken by the Patriots. "In a frolick," a sergeant and two soldiers visited his home in March 1778 to arrest him for treasonable conduct. He invited them in to eat and drink. Suddenly, he grabbed one of their guns and fired. One of the soldiers was killed instantly, and the second died a few days later.

Hill fled to the woods and swamps, where he remained in hiding for four months before fleeing to a British vessel.

CHENEY CLOW

By April, a Delaware Tory named Cheney Clow had had enough of the Patriots and the disruptions they had caused. Deciding to stand up for what he thought was right, he gathered together about 150 of the "disaffected" in Little Creek Hundred, Kent County, where they built a "fort," apparently a sort of stockade. Armed with "guns, swords, pistols, bayonets, clubs and other instruments of war," to use the language of Clow's subsequent indictment for treason, they seemed formidable. Concerned that they would march on Dover, a detachment of Delaware militia commanded by Lieutenant Colonel Charles Pope was sent to investigate. Pope's men seem to have exchanged fire with the fort's occupants and then left. Returning two days later with reinforcements, Pope found the post abandoned and destroyed it.[138]

On April 24, 1778, Caesar Rodney reported to Henry Laurence:

> *I, as soon as possible, collected and sent about one hundred and forty of the Militia of this County, under the Command of Lieutenant Colonel Pope of the Delaware against them. The insurgents had built a Fort which the Militia Surrounded on the Thursday night following but Mr Clow and his gang, hearing of their approach fled. The Militia burnt the fort and secured all the stolen effects in in and about it and Returned. I then fitted out a number of horsemen, since when many of them have been taken and others Surrendered…[the] Single men are sent off with a recruiting party of the Delaware Regiment to enlist…. This infernal set are, I believe, broke up, and hope to hear in a few days that the Villain Clow is taken,*
>
> *I am Sir Yr Most Ob't Humble Srvt.*
> *Caesar Rodney.*[139]
> *Carlisle Commission*

The British Carlisle Commissioners arrived from England and, on May 4, sailed up the Delaware to New Castle aboard the *Trident*. Here they were astounded to discover that the British did not control the riverbanks:

Bombay Hook. *Karen Sinar Dever.*

[T]*o our great surprise all the naval armament collected together with evident preparation for the immediate evacuation of Philadelphia by his Majesty's forces. Every vessel of war was recalled from the coast, and the transports, etc., which we passed, to the amount of near four hundred, were filled with the miserable inhabitants of that city whose attachment to our cause obliged them to risk their fortunes with us or swear allegiance to the Congress. The enemy were suffered to act in the most offensive manner under the guns of our ships of war. No boat was permitted by the inhabitants of either side to approach the shore. No fresh provisions were furnished to the sick. And as we passed…were insulted by a party of riflemen who fired several shots at us, which, though striking at too great a distance to occasion the least alarm, yet manifested the malevolence as well as rashness of their intentions.*[140]

On May 6, the commissioners reached New Castle, where they received a note from Howe, who was sending an armed sloop to bring them to Philadelphia. British general Clinton had been ordered to evacuate Philadelphia one month before the commissioners left England due to changing strategic priorities after France's entry into the war. Carlisle angrily wrote to his wife that the administration wanted the commission to be "a mixture of ridicule, nullity, and embarrassments." Among Carlisle's commissioners was William Eden, 1st Baron Auckland, head of the British spies in Europe. Eden was very upset that he hadn't been informed of the evacuation orders. Carlisle was of the opinion that the administration had done this intentionally, since the commissioners might not otherwise have left England.

As it became clear that the British were ending their occupation of Philadelphia, the Continental Congress sent for the Quaker prisoners to be brought north from Virginia to Lancaster, Pennsylvania. Negotiations were now opened to exchange Delaware's former president McKinly for William Franklin, Loyalist governor of New Jersey.[141]

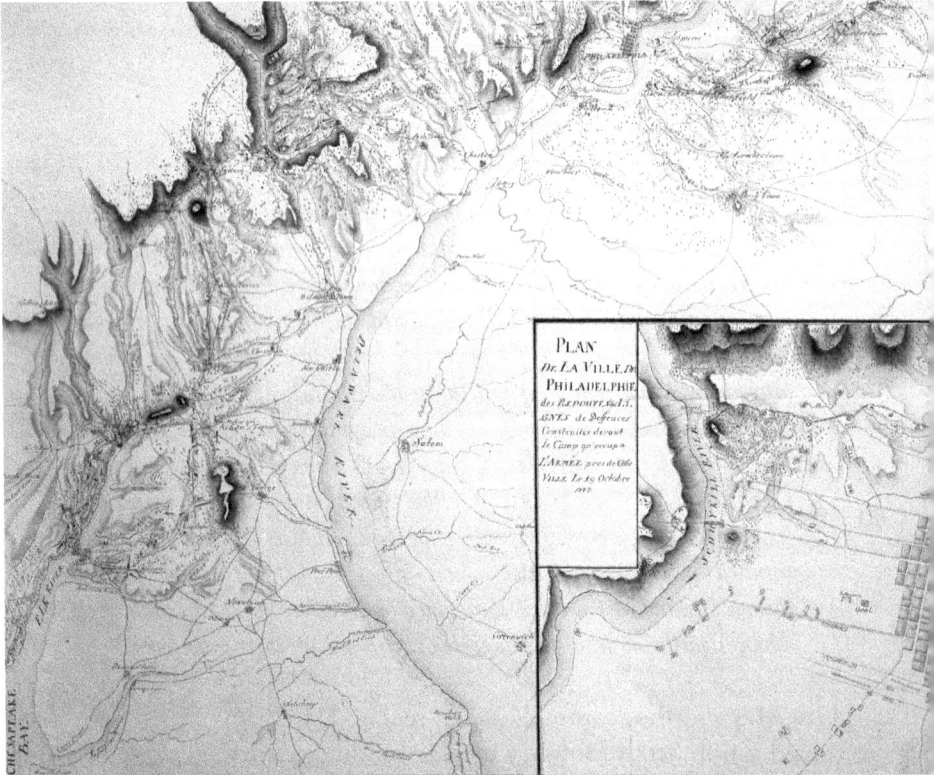

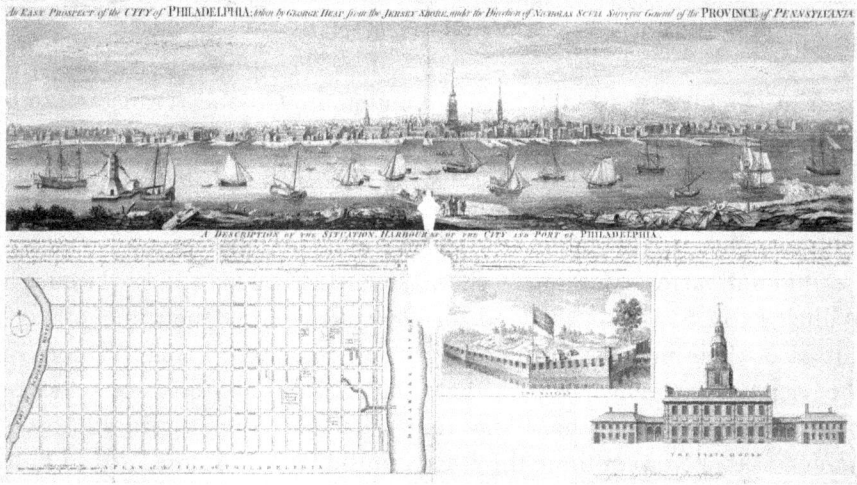

Above: Philadelphia. *Society of Cincinnati.*

Below: Map of Philadelphia Campaign. *Wikimedia Commons.*

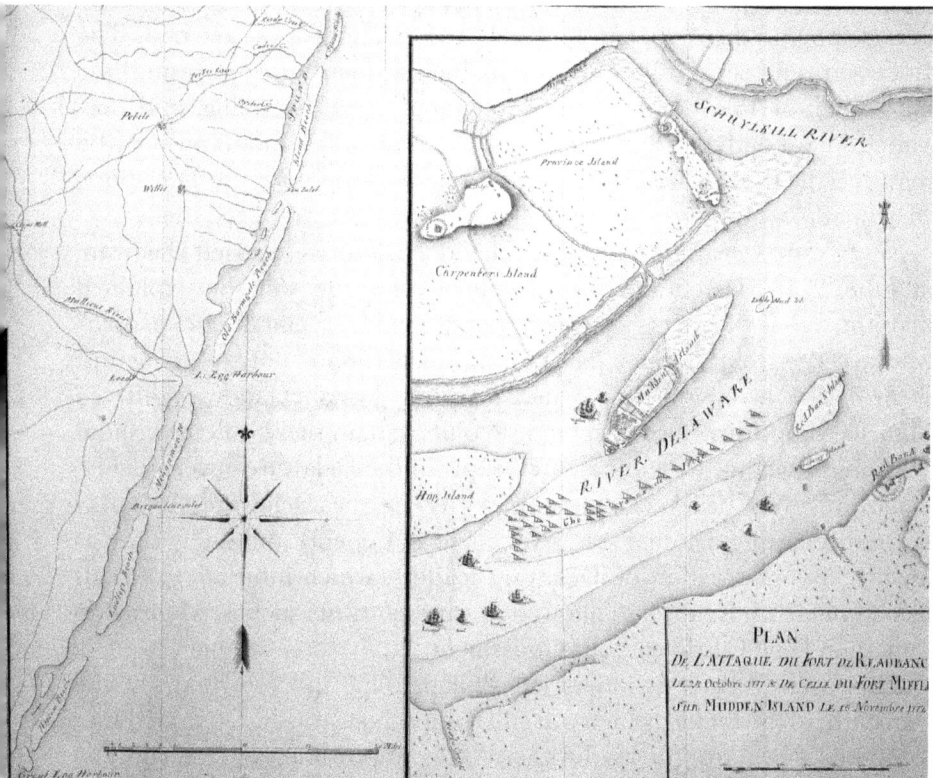

Evacuation

In May, George Washington sent Lieutenant Colonel François-Louis Teissèdre, Marquis de Fleury, to Wilmington as a division inspector. Two of Smallwood's officers were to be appointed as brigade inspectors and receive from Colonel de Fleury the written instructions relative to the most elementary points of drill and maneuvering composed by the Continental army's famous drill master, the Prussian-born Friedrich Wilhelm von Steuben. They, in turn, would instruct the other officers and they their men. Washington wrote to Smallwood that "to correct the vicious step which our soldiers have contracted and introduce a natural march easy to the soldier and calculated to gain ground, it will be necessary to discontinue the use of music for some time."[142] On June 9, 1778, Smallwood's brigade of Delaware and Maryland troops began arriving in Valley Forge, and almost simultaneously, about three hundred British merchant ships and transports anchored near Reedy Island.

On June 16, reports came that women and children were embarking on board transports in the Delaware River and that British officers were removing the sick from hospitals and weapons from arsenals. The distressed refugees on these ships remained at their anchorage until the third week of the month. Their food supply was dwindling, and they waited impatiently for a signal to sail. Commissioner Eden, on board a ship with the fleet, noted, "Crowds of wretched families in the Transports all around us are incredible—it will not be easy for us to feed them."

New Castle's wealthiest Loyalist, Theodore Maurice, also left Delaware in June 1778. Defending his allegiance after the war, he explained that the rebel "leaders were his friends and very moderate people" who accepted him "under parole in point of honor not to act against them." The leading Pennsylvania Loyalist, Joseph Galloway, offered Maurice supporting testimony: one "could remain there quietly without trimming—as they were moderate people in the Delaware government." Galloway even believed that a majority in the Delaware Assembly favored retaining colonial status yet could not openly and safely state as much. The moderation of Delaware leaders, which infuriated radicals like Thomas McKean, had allowed passive Loyalists such as Maurice to remain in New Castle without harassment.[143]

The Carlisle commissioners left Philadelphia and returned, on the sixteenth, to the *Trident*, which was still lying at New Castle. Commissioner William Eden wrote to his brother, "It is impossible, to give you any adequate idea of the vast scale of this country. I know little more of it than I saw in 150 miles up the Delaware; but I know enough to regret most heartily that our rulers instead of making the tour of Europe did not finish their education by a voyage round the coasts and rivers of the western side of the Atlantic."[144]

The British evacuation of Philadelphia began at four o'clock in the morning. A party of the American cavalry pursued them closely and took many prisoners, some of whom were refugees. By the afternoon of June 18, most of the British army was gone from Philadelphia. Captain Allen McLane's company of Delaware light infantry slipped into the city just as the last British patrols were leaving and captured a few officers who had dallied too long with their "tender acquaintances." Otherwise, the Americans found "nothing but empty redoubts and houses." Military supplies had been removed or destroyed, dwellings looted and merchant ships burned at the wharves." Soon after the evacuation, Major General Benedict Arnold (still an American Patriot at this point) took possession of Philadelphia.[145]

The Delaware Continental Regiment participated in the June 28, 1778 Battle of Monmouth Court House in New Jersey. After Monmouth, it marched White Plains, New York. Although the British had moved on, in Delaware tension remained high. A British naval vessel remained on guard at Cape Henlopen, and small boats operating under its protection both raided and traded with area farmers. By July 1, 1778, all white males in Delaware had been asked to pledge loyalty to the Patriot cause. Quakers and Tories who refused to take this oath soon became scapegoats, and their property was seized.

MIXED ALLEGIANCE

On July 2, 1778, Congress returned to Philadelphia, and the following week, French admiral d'Estaing's fleet arrived in Delaware before moving on to New York. Caesar Rodney wrote to William Patterson on July 11, "As the enemy have now entirely left the Delaware, and [with] a large French fleet on our Coast, there does not appear to be that danger to this State [as] when [the assembly] passed the Act for establishing the independent company you were commissioned to command...Therefore, the said Independent Company for the County of New Castle is hereby disbanded."[146]

The mixed allegiance of Delawareans in all three counties, as well as the relative lenience of the Delaware government, is showcased in the *Act of Free Pardon and Oblivion*, issued on June 26, 1778, as the British withdrew from Philadelphia. As the main theater of war shifted away from the Delaware Valley, the state confiscated the estates of forty-six confirmed Loyalists, although most of those who had asked

Infantry: Continental Army, 1779–1783. Lithograph by G.H. Buek & Company, New York. H.A. Ogden, artist. *Library of Congress.*

for pardon for actively aiding the British were excused. The General Assembly recorded a number of cases like the following:

> *Barcus, James and Barcus, Stephen, Loyalists. Little Creek Hundred. Husbandmen Excepted from Pardon, indicted for an attempted rebellion in April 1778, having on this and other occasions assembled large quantities of arms and stolen goods and munitions from peaceful citizens. On payment of the costs of prosecution, James Barcus, along with Stephen Barcas, William Burrows, and Samuel Hatfield, all husbandmen. Were freed in July 1778. Upon payment of costs of prosecution, Presley Allee and Simeon Van Winkle were freed. Excepted from Pardon. John Brinckle, a Loyalist from Dover Hundred. A shallopman who was Excepted from Pardon. He was indicted for selling corn to British vessels in 1777 and freed upon costs of prosecution in July 1778.* [147]

In August, former state president John McKinly was paroled by the British in exchange for William Franklin, former governor of New Jersey.

In October 1778, a large shipment of shoes and military clothing arrived from France. Quartermaster Nathanael Greene distributed them to the different states by lottery. Virginia, Delaware, Pennsylvania, Massachusetts, New Hampshire and Hazen's Canadians received brown coats. In the second lottery, Delaware also got some blue coats. These uniforms were described by Continental clothier George Measam as being of good-quality cloth, lined with white serge (finer wool), and included white waistcoats and breeches. The brown linen breeches were made for knee buckles, which were not supplied. Coats were well cut, being large and warm, with the lapels made to button over the breast and belly; the buttons were made of silver-colored metal. The jacket's sleeve cuffs were designed to be buttoned.[148]

VOTING

Henry Laurens had succeeded John Hancock as president of Continental Congress. He pleaded with Delaware to "supply immediately a proper number of Representatives in Congress [as] for some considerable time past the State has been almost wholly unrepresented." As early as June, Thomas McKean had urged for the same thing. The most pressing issue at hand was to get at least some form of the Articles of Confederation passed.[149] In Delaware, the major concerns about congressional issues included the apportioning of the rapidly growing wartime debt and figuring out a way to protect the small state from being outvoted by larger states. Laurens, pressed for Delaware's decision, reminded Caesar Rodney that out of all the Thirteen Colonies, only Delaware and Maryland had not made a decision locally to accept the Articles of Confederation. Rodney called for an emergency meeting on Monday, November 23, but it was not until February that Delaware authorized the federal legislation.

Chapter 11

COLD AND HUNGRY

Morristown and More

F rom December 1778 to June 1779, the Delaware Continental Regiment was positioned with the main portion of the army along the base of the Watchung Mountains, in Somerset County, New Jersey. From this position, they could threaten the British garrison in New York, and if the need arose, they would be able to protect New Jersey and quickly reinforce the Hudson Highlands. The fall and winter of 1778–79 lacked action and was a time of transition. Lafayette briefly returned home to France to lobby for additional French military support.[150]

PROHIBITIONS

In February 1779, the Dover Assembly, in an attempt to reserve grain for the use of soldiers, made a very controversial decision, prohibiting the distilling of whiskey and any other spirits from wheat, rye or any other sort of grain, meal or flour. This restriction would begin on March 1 and was to continue until July of the following year:

> *Persons acting contrary to the directions of this act, or the person or persons in whose custody or possession any such tun, washbatch, cask, copper still, or other vessel or utensil made use of contrary to the intention of this act be found, shall respectively for every such offense forfeit and pay the sum*

of two hundred pounds and incur also a forfeiture of the value of all such wheat, rye, barley or other grain and all such flour and meal, whiskey and other spirits and of all such stills, vessels or other utensils, to be ascertained and assisized by the Jury by whom the cause shall be tried.[151]

Upstate, Wilmington Friends Meeting received word that week that political prisoner Jehu Hollingsworth had been released from the Lancaster jail. Joseph West was assigned to look into Hollingsworth's needs and condition and report at the next meeting. By the end of February, no information was yet available.

Wilmington had barely recovered from the British and American occupations when cavalrymen under the command of Casimir Pulaski—a Polish nobleman, soldier and American military commander—came to town. Pulaski had fought bravely at Brandywine and Germantown, and he had spent the winter of 1777–78 at Valley Forge. On February 2, 1779, Washington ordered Pulaski and his men to the southern front, where they would arrive in Charleston, South Carolina, on May 8. The *American Watchman* gave an account of his regiment's stay in Wilmington:

After the British left us…we had Pulaski's Regiment quartered in this Town, on their way to the South—probably to Savannah (where the commander lost his life storming that fortress.). While those troops continued with us, which was but a short time, a circumstance took place that agitated my feelings very much. From want of barracks, the soldiers were "billeted" upon the citizens, and among them was Richard Carson, an old and respectable citizen. The whole regiment were in my eyes a formidable and indeed terrific race of men. They were all horse troops, who wore mustachios, and large bearskin caps standing a foot above their heads. They walked with long swords that railed the ground as they walked. When the soldiers came to Richard Carson's to introduce the officer who was to reside in his house, the old man met them at the door, and refused entrance—and a warm struggle took place. He standing astride of the whole entrance, with his arms spread to each door post—his two daughters pulling at his back to get him into the house and the horsemen in front struggling to gain admittance. In the contest, the old man's wig was thrown under foot and he stood manfully, with his bald pate exposed, not at all daunted. They continued for some time, until a soldier taking his sword by the blade, struck the old man over the bare head with the hilt and knocked

The Delaware Blue Hens, Delaware Continental Regiment. Paul Catts, artist.

him down—when they entered triumphantly. Whether they used or abused their victory, I do not now remember—but the circumstances remained very vividly imprinted on my memory for a long time, as one of the most distressing scenes I had witnessed.[152]

Pulaski and his men rendered great services during the Siege of Savannah. On October 9, while attempting to rally troops for a cavalry charge, Pulaski was mortally wounded by grapeshot, and died two days later.

WARNINGS

On May 12, 1779, the Delaware Continental Regiment was reorganized into nine companies and assigned to the 2nd Maryland Brigade of the main Continental army under Colonel William Gist and Major General Johann de Kalb.[153] Throughout the spring, the Delaware troops' nerves were on edge. On May 18, a remonstrance signed by fifteen officers stationed in Middlebrook, New Jersey, announced the Delaware Continental Regiment's intention of withdrawing from service to the army unless provisions were made for its necessary supplies.

Meanwhile, George Washington received a letter from Christiana, Delaware, from Samuel Patterson, brigadier general of Delaware militia and first treasurer of Delaware State, warning him about Jacob Moore, a former assemblyman and Sussex County lawyer who wanted a pass to go to New York. Moore was the same person who had drawn a sword on the men who had tried to arrest Thomas Robinson several years before:

From Samuel Patterson, Delaware State Christeen, May 30th 1779

A Gentleman waited on me to day to Inform me that our President, had Given a pass, or recommendation to your Excellency to go into New York to a Certain Jacob Moore Esqr. Atterney at Lewis Town in this state. I thought it my duty to inform you as well as to my Country he is said to be a dangerous man in our grand Struggle and by no means should he [be] suffered to go in under any pretence.[154]

On June 30, at the end of the legislative session, after the majority of both houses agreed to give Caesar Rodney the power to impose martial law, they had adjourned without doing so. Samuel Patterson was appalled. As in the case of Jacob Moore, Patterson wanted martial law to prevent known Loyalists from going to New York to help the British:

I never was so deceived in my politics, as on yesterday.... To my great surprise, when every moment I and others expected its appearance, the Notice was, the Assembly was, adjourned. Nothing can be done without it. I am tired of such complacency and am almost determined never more to appear in that public body who cannot see the necessity of spirited measures. [155]

Receiving word of potential trouble, Washington ordered "Light-Horse Harry" Lee (father of Robert E. Lee) to provide reconnaissance. One of Lee's men, Allen McLane from Smyrna, Delaware, entered Stony Point, New York, on July 2 disguised as a "simple countryman." McLane took careful note of the fortifications and strength of the British garrison and reported back.

Allen McLane (1746–1829). *Delaware Public Archives.*

Anthony Wayne—with 1,350 men, including soldiers from the Delaware Continental Regiment—soon attacked Stony Point in a victorious nighttime raid. One month later, McLane and his dragoons participated in the bayonet charge at Paulus Hook. Charging at four o'clock in the morning, the Americans won without firing a shot.

WINTER AT MORRISTOWN

The Delaware Continental Regiment saw little action during the remainder of 1779 and wintered at Morristown, New Jersey. Early in the encampment, on December 4, the Delaware officers at Morristown signed an "address" thanking the Delaware Assembly for its generosity but complaining because they had not "yet received but two months of the supplies allowed and have no prospect of receiving any more, as Captain Craighead [the state clothier] has received but 1,400 pounds to purchase a quarterly supply of necessaries," which sum was "inadequate to the purpose." On December 18, Washington wrote to Caesar Rodney, the president of Delaware, and to the governors of New York, Pennsylvania, New Jersey and Maryland, "The situation of the army with respect to supplies is beyond description. It has been five or six weeks passed on half allowance…our magazines are absolutely empty everywhere and our commissaries entirely destitute of money."[156]

There were more than seven thousand soldiers encamped with Washington at Morristown, New Jersey, during the "hard winter." In January 1780, the temperature rose above freezing only once, and there was "one of the most tremendous snowstorms ever remembered." Tents were blown away, and the men did not have warm clothes. For many years afterward, when people spoke of the "hard winter," it was that winter they had in mind. One private claimed that some bark gnawed from a twig was the only thing he had eaten in four days. In January, Major John Patten of Dover wrote to Caesar Rodney from Morristown:

> *The Army has been reduced to most extreme want for provisions, having subsist five days on half a pound of salt beef and half a pint of rice without any other kind of support whatever…On the 17th an Inspection Return of the Cloathing in Captain Pattan's Company, Thirty-nine men were inspected. All of them had coats and waistcoats; all but one had a shirt apiece, and 11 princes of privilege had each another shirt. All but two had hats and either stockings or socks. But 19 had neither breeches nor "wooling overalls," perhaps they were luxuriating in linen trousers, so suitable for zero weather, perhaps not. And 26 had no blankets.*[157]

The assembly quickly responded, voting £15,000 sterling to purchase supplies for their relief. State clothier Captain George Craighead reported the following month that his task was

> [y]*et not quite complete, as there was not the articles, which they wanted in the Public Stores: (Which are 200 pairs woolen overalls and 70 blankets), nor know I how to get them. I could not get to purchase white broad cloth for waist coats and breeches, except a few yards at 600 dollars (which I declined). Major John Patten also reported that "our regiment is rather better clothed than any in the army."*[158]

It was perhaps not too surprising that Colonel David Hall, who had been wounded at Germantown and suffered with his men at Morristown, resigned his commission. When the Delaware Continental Regiment went to South Carolina in May 1780, Hall did not go.

Major John André (1750–1780). *Library of Congress.*

A regiment of Delaware militia was called into service alongside the Continental army in the summer of 1780. Commanded by Lieutenant Colonel Henry Neill, this militia regiment served in northern New Jersey and along the Hudson River, at Dobbs Ferry, New York. In September, British major John André, who had been in Delaware during the Battle of Cooch's Bridge, was condemned as a spy, and on October 2, 1780, members of the Delaware militia unit witnessed his hanging at Tappan, New York.

As their contracts would soon expire, Neill's men were sent to Philadelphia to be discharged, from which place they were sent home on October 22. One of them recalled later:

He enlisted in the army of the United States at Newport, Delaware, in the latter end of July, 1780, with Captain Robinson and served in the Second Delaware of the line under the following named officers. Declarant and four others, his companions all from Chester County were by the same time enlisted by the said Captain William Robinson at Newport in the State of Delaware and engaged to serve for one year unless sooner discharged. That he and his comrades, under the command of Captain William McClements of Dover, were marched from Newport to Wilmington and were there registered and sized, and in Wilmington was appointed orderly sergeant. From thence were transported by water to Philadelphia. Our regiment was commanded by Colonel. Henry Neale [sic] and we had one Major, viz., Maj. James Mitchell of Dagsboro, Sussex, Delaware and then to Trenton, Princeton, Brunswick, Troytown, Morristown, Hackensack, Dobbs Ferry—main army at Tappan.[159]

George Washington ordered Baron de Kalb to take the Delaware Continental Regiment and Maryland Continental Line to the Carolinas. Captain Robert Kirkwood noted in his journal on May 8 that De Kalb left from "the Head of Elk, in Compy with 50 sail of vessels, being the Second Brigade of the Maryland Line. Destined for Petersburgh, Virginia, at which Port the vessel I was in. Arrived the 23 Inst." On July 25, Kirkwood wrote, "This Day the Honble. Majr. Genl Gates arrived and took command of all the Southern Troops."[160]

A-Digging Graves They Told Me

In the spring of 1780, the Delaware Continentals were sent to the southern theater. On August 13, 1780, Gates led De Kalb's men—who were suffering from heat, humidity, scurvy and diarrhea—toward Camden, South Carolina. On August 16, British forces under General Cornwallis routed the American forces of Major General Horatio Gates about five miles north of Camden, South Carolina, strengthening the British hold on the Carolinas. The rout was a humiliating defeat for Gates, the American general best known for commanding the Americans at the British defeat of Saratoga. After Camden, the Delaware Continental Regiment was reorganized on two different occasions—first being divided into two companies and then being divided into three companies of light infantry with troops from Maryland. The 3rd Company, commanded by Captain Robert Kirkwood, consisted mainly of Delawareans.[161]

It was under General Nathanael Greene, who took command of the Southern Department in the fall of 1780, that the Delaware Continental Regiment made its

Haslet's Delaware Regiment

Delaware Continental soldier.
Delaware Historical Society.

most effective contributions as a fighting force. Through a long series of battles—Cowpens, Guilford Court House, Eutaw Springs, Ninety-Six and Hobkirk's Hill—that ultimately forced the British to surrender in the South, the Delawareans performed with exceptional courage and skill and earned the esteem of the highest commanders. Of the Delaware Continentals, Richard Henry Lee later wrote, "The state of Delaware produced one regiment only and certainly no regiment in the army surpassed it in soldiership."[162]

Chapter 12

CUT DOWN ALIVE

A cross the colonies, ordinary citizens were suffering and complaining. A Hessian officer, Major Baurmeister, saw a devastated America in 1780:

> *Everybody is disillusioned, and a disastrous indecision undermines all the American provinces. No matter how this war may end, as long as this mess continues, the people suffer at the hands of both friend and foe. The Americans rob them of their earnings and cattle, and we burn their empty houses; and in moments of sensitiveness, it is difficult to decide which party is more cruel. These cruelties have begotten enough misery to last an entire generation.*[163]

In 1780, a summer drought destroyed most of the wheat harvest. Already resentful of the tax burden imposed on them by the war, many farmers were forced into destitution and unable to pay those taxes. In Sussex County, the Black Camp Rebellion was a reaction of unhappy residents of Cedar Creek and Broadkill Hundred to the hardships caused by the War of Independence. About four hundred men formed in "[a]ssociations to fight against Whigs because taxes was two [*sic*] high and no man could live by such laws."[164]

In researching tax and probate records, historian Harold Hancock discovered that many Black Camp Loyalists were small landowners, poor farmers frustrated over the situation the war had left them in; none had ever held any position of prominence, and almost half of them signed their name with an *X*. They congregated for almost a month in a swamp near

Ellendale until the Kent County Militia arrested them. Some were sent to serve in the Continental army, and thirty-seven were indicted for treason by the Delaware Supreme Court. A jury of ordinary citizens concluded that one of the Black Camp tax protestors, Seagoe Potter, had been "seduced by the instigation of the Devil" into opposing the government. The jurors found Potter and seven others guilty of treason and told him:

> *It is considered by the Court that you, Seagoe Potter, return to the prison from whence you came, from thence you must be drawn to the place of execution. When you come there you must be hanged by the neck but not till you be dead, for you must be cut down alive, then your bowels must be taken out and burnt before your face, then your head must be severed from your body, and your body divided into four quarters, and these must be at the disposal of the Supreme authority of the State.*[165]

After having seriously frightened the participants, the General Assembly pardoned them on November 4, 1780. Upstate, the Quaker Book of Sufferings showed increased activity during this same period. Demands on the White Clay Creek Quakers and others were increasing. So-called officials were raiding their homes and taking things in lieu of war taxes. Daniel Byrnes, whose home had been commandeered for a Council of War in September 1777, was especially hard hit:

> *1780. From Daniel Byrnes by virtue of execution from James Black by James Carr Constable at the suit of William McClay capt., demand not known, one case of drawers. 1780. From Daniel Byrnes by Thomas Wallace collector for war tax demand not known, 3 barrels of flour. 1781. From Daniel Byrnes by a number of armed men 31 bushels of shorts and by McGhee Constable by execution from James Blake [sic, Black] and Evan Reece for demand of 45/4 the remainder of a supply tax after the price of shorts was deducted and 23/1 demand for bounty tax three barrels of superfine flour and by Robert Wallace collector for war tax one barrel of superfine flour.*

It is interesting to note that James Black was not only the sheriff but also a miller in direct competition with Byrnes and the son-in-law of local militia leader, Christiana miller Samuel Patterson.[166]

1781: Articles of Confederation

Although representatives had been meeting together and developing policies and procedures since the first protests against the Stamp Act began in 1764, Continental Congress was, in many ways, an ad hoc committee. On March 1, 1781, five years after the Declaration of Independence, the Articles of Confederation were finally ratified, creating an official government for the United States with a loose confederation of sovereign states. Although this act provided some official guidelines for collective action, it did not solve the burgeoning fiscal crisis.

In the early months of 1781, as the war's action shifted to the southern states, life in Delaware was relatively quiet. American paper money by now was totally worthless. Congress had printed $200 million of the "Continentals" backed by nothing but the promise of eventual victory. Only hard money— coin of the French, Dutch, English or Spanish realms—was being accepted by most merchants and farmers. John Yeates, deputy quartermaster of the Continental army, later noted that "considerable movement of the

John Dickinson's house at Jones Neck, Kent County, Delaware. *Delaware Public Archives.*

Army going on Southward [was] a circumstance from real necessity productive of the most Disagreable occurences, the taking of property indiscriminately which never fails of giving much distress, and causing just murmuring."[167]

The Delaware Continental Regiment fought bravely at Cowpens, South Carolina, in January and would play a starring role throughout the Southern Campaign, but thousands of other soldiers would be streaming through Delaware for the rest of the year. On the national front, the good work that Lafayette had done in negotiating with the French government for assistance and official involvement had come to fruition. French general Rochambeau and French troops were now marching south from Rhode Island to join the American forces in Dobbs Ferry, New York. On March 2, 1781, Under Washington's orders, Lafayette and 1,500 advance forces arrived in Christiana, Delaware, with cannons, stores and ammunition, headed south to Virginia to unite forces with Von Steuben, who was already there.

On July 10, Thomas McKean was elected president of the Continental Congress. By August, frustrated Tories, angry about deprivations caused by a war they did not support, landed at Kitts Hummock in Kent County and marched to Jones Neck. There they plundered John Dickinson's plantation, taking chests of silver, salt meat, bottles of wine and bedclothes to the value of £1,500 pounds. By the time the sheriff and militia arrived from Dover, the intruders were gone.[168]

Chapter 13

THE YORKTOWN CAMPAIGN

In July and August 1781, Continental army troops commanded by General George Washington were encamped in and near Dobbs Ferry, New York, alongside allied French forces under the command of the Comte de Rochambeau. On August 14, 1781, a communication was received from French admiral Comte de Grasse in the West Indies advocating a joint land and sea attack against the British in Virginia. Washington and Rochambeau's men now began a march of more than four hundred miles from Dobbs Ferry to the Chesapeake region of Virginia. Predominant among the troops passing across New Castle County, Delaware, on their way from Marcus Hook, Pennsylvania, to Elkton, Maryland, were the 1st Rhode Island Regiment, Scammel's Light Infantry and the 1st and 2nd New Jersey.[169]

VOICES OF THE PAST

Thousands of soldiers, horses, cattle and baggage trains followed the twenty-six-mile transportation corridor across New Castle County. Today, that system of old roads is marked as part of the nine-state, D.C. and France Yorktown Campaign Trail, now known as the Washington-Rochambeau Revolutionary Route (W3R-NHT). Entering Delaware at the Marcus Hook-Claymont border, they rumbled ten miles down Philadelphia Pike, through

Robinson House, Claymont. *Ray Hester.*

Brandywine Village and Wilmington, turning west onto today's Maryland Avenue, passing through Newport and Stanton, down old Stanton-Christina Road to Christiana Village and past Iron Hill on their way to the Head of Elk in Maryland. Many eyewitness accounts still exist.

New Englander Samuel Benjamin's journal for September 5 notes, "Set sail and reached Cristeen about twelve o'clock, when we disembarked and marched about one mile, and joined the regiment and marched four miles that afternoon to Iron Hill."[170]

On September 6, 1781, Samuel Tallmadge of Brookhaven, Suffolk County, New York, noted that his troop entered Delaware from Camp Marcus Hook:

> *Embarked about six o'clock. Continued our march down to Wilmington passed by the town, and proceeded on to Newport there halted half an hour then continued our march to Christeen Bridge where we arrived about one o'clock and encamped. Wilmington and Newport is situated on Christeen Creek, the latter in Delaware State.*[171]

Enos Reeves, born in Cumberland County, New Jersey, elaborated on the view from Brandywine Village to Wilmington:

Brandywine Village. *David Ames, HABS-HAER, CHAD, Library of Congress.*

This Creek [Brandywine] *is famous all over America for its Merchant Mills, seven of them being built within 150 yards of each other—and the vessels load and unload at the mills. Wilmington is a fine borough, has a number of regular streets, a Court House, market house, and contains about 50 or 60 houses, a number of which are very good—with a fine Academy on the hill. You may have a beautiful prospect of the town from the Delaware, as it is built on a hill side, and from the town a beautiful prospect of the Christiana Creek.* [172]

And Joseph Plumb Martin of western Massachusetts described arriving in Newport, Delaware, with a boatload of gunpowder:

A part of our men, with myself, went down the Delaware River in a schooner which had her hold nearly full of gunpowder.... I did not feel very agreeably, I confess...with such a quantity of powder under my feet...but no accident happened and we made it down the river to the mouth of the Christiana Creek up which we were bound. We were compelled to anchor here on account of wind and tide. Here we passed an uneasy night from fear of British cruisers, several of which were in the bay. In the morning we got under weigh [sic], *the wind serving, and proceeded up the creek fourteen miles, the creek passing, the most of its course through a marsh, as crooked as a snake in motion. There was one place in particular, near the village of Newport where you sail miles to gain about forty rods. We went on till the vessel grounded for lack of water. We then lightened her by taking out a part of her cargo, and when the tide came in we got up to the wharves and left her at the disposal of the artillerists.* [173]

Shannon Inn, Historic Christiana. *Delaware Public Archives.*

Samuel Tallmadge noted in his journal from Christiana on September 7, 1781, that "about 7 oclock in the morning the French army marched through this place." He continued on Saturday, September 8, 1781, "Part of the army was constantly imployed in loading and transporting ammunition together with other stores to the Head of Elk." The next day, "at beating of Reavellee we struck camp and marched to the Head of Elk and encamped."[174]

Captains McKennan and Quenoualt's companies—with eighty-five men, seventy-five new recruits and ten veterans—were assigned to duties in Virginia. A fleet of small boats was waiting at Head of Elk to convey the joint forces down the Chesapeake and into Virginia. At the same time, Kirkwood and Jaquett's men remained stationed in South Carolina.

Kirkwood, still posted in South Carolina, "received Intillegence of the Surrender of Lord Cornwaliss whole Army to this Excellency Genl Washington in York Town."[175] On October 19, 1781, Cornwallis's army had surrendered to the joint French and American forces at Yorktown, Virginia.

Chapter 14

HOMEWARD BOUND

B ringing an official message to the president of the Continental Congress
from George Washington in Yorktown, Maryland's Lieutenant Colonel
Tench Tilghman arrived in Philadelphia on October 24. Washington's
letter to McKean was deliberately low-key, stating that that "a reduction
of the British Army under the command of Lord Cornwallis is most
happily effected." Washington hoped that the president and Congress "will
be pleased to accept my congratulations on this happy event." Later that
afternoon, dressed in full uniform, Tilghman formally announced the news
to the members of Congress. That evening, a torchlight celebration was held
in Philadelphia in honor of the victory at Yorktown.

Three days later, the *Minutes of the Council of the Delaware State* recorded:

> *Whereas it is expected that General Washington with a part of the army*
> *under his command, will shortly pass through this State by the post at*
> *Christiana, in New Castle County, there was an immediate need to supply*
> *that post with such provisions and forage as may be wanting on that*
> *occasion.…… [A budget] not exceeding the sum of one thousand pounds,*
> *specie, in its value was earmarked for this expense, with the directive that*
> *the General Assembly will, before its rising, provide ways and means for the*
> *discharge of the debts.*[176]

Somehow it seems very fitting that on November 13, 1781, John Dickinson
was inaugurated as the new president of the Delaware State. His *Letters from a*

Surrender of Cornwallis. Published by N. Currier, circa 1846. Lithograph shows Major General O'Hara handing his sword in surrender while surrounded by French and American soldiers. *Library of Congress.*

Farmer had been published nearly twenty years before, and he had worked on the Olive Branch Petition and many other official documents. When negotiations failed, Dickinson had served as both a soldier and a statesman for all these many years. As the war ended, President Dickinson accepted his new position, saying:

> *May a happy harmony, in sentiment and measures, so beneficial to society, always prevail among us, or, if there must be division, let it only be between those who generously contend for the freedom, independence, and prosperity of their country, and such as weakly wish for a dangerous and dishonorable submission to enemies so infatuated as to hate where they ought to admire and to provoke their own and pursue the ruin of these states, though nature and policy point out that we should "be blessings one to another."*[177]

By the end of November 1781, thousands of soldiers were passing through Delaware. Samuel Benjamin, who had marched through Delaware on his way south, now documented his return trip: "March from Head of Elk to within one mile and a half from Wilmington." And the following

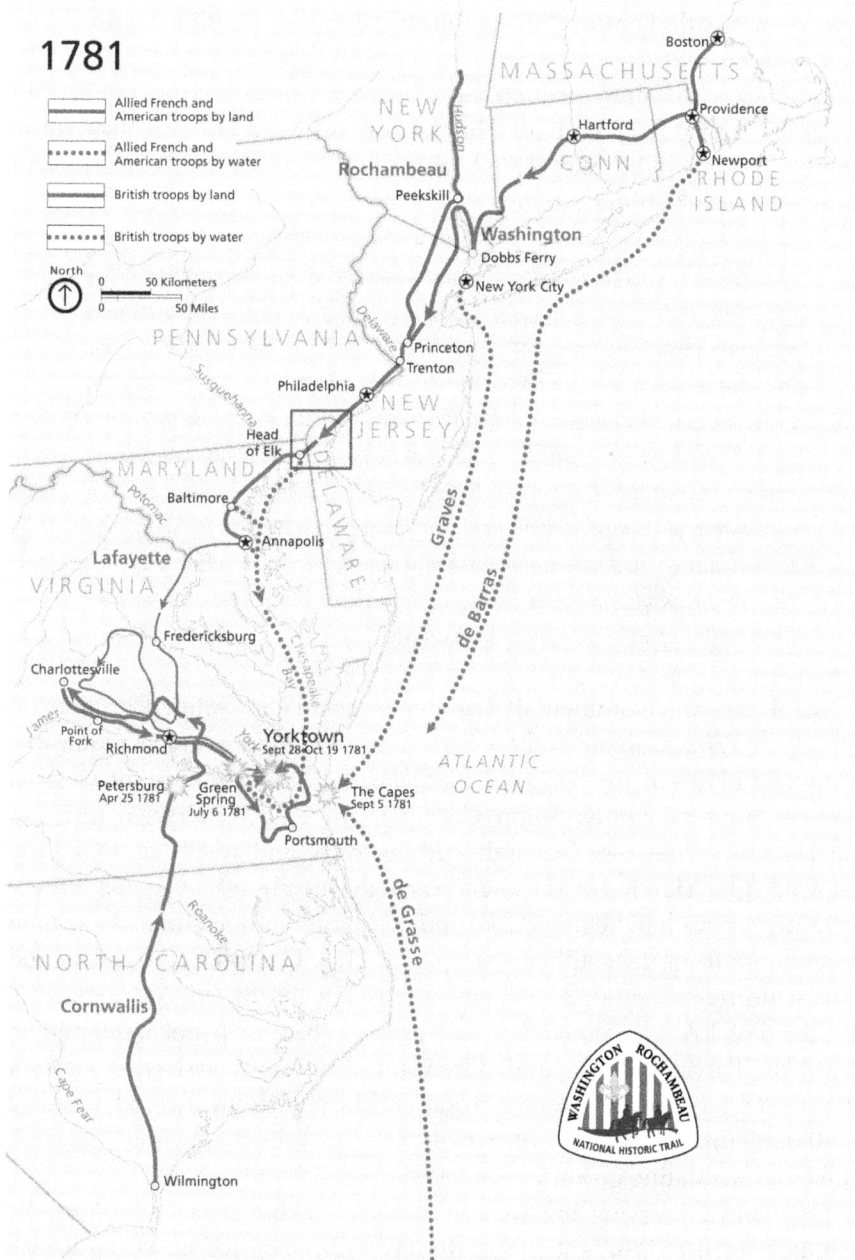

1781

Allied French and
American troops by land

Allied French and
American troops by water

British troops by land

British troops by water

North

0   50 Kilometers

0   50 Miles

MASSACHUSETTS

Boston

NEW
YORK

Providence

Hartford

CONN

Newport

RHODE
ISLAND

Rochambeau

Peekskill

Washington

Dobbs Ferry

New York City

Hudson

PENNSYLVANIA

Princeton

Trenton

Philadelphia

Delaware

NEW
JERSEY

Head
of Elk

MARYLAND

DELAWARE

Baltimore

Potomac

Susquehanna

Annapolis

Graves

de Barras

Lafayette

VIRGINIA

Fredericksburg

Charlottesville

James

Point of
Fork

Richmond

Petersburg
Apr 25 1781

Green
Spring
July 6 1781

Yorktown
Sept 28-Oct 19 1781

The Capes
Sept 5 1781

Chesapeake Bay

York

ATLANTIC
OCEAN

Portsmouth

NORTH CAROLINA

Roanoke

de Grasse

Cornwallis

Cape Fear

WASHINGTON ROCHAMBEAU

NATIONAL HISTORIC TRAIL

Wilmington

Washington-Rochambeau National Historic Trail.

day, "New Castle County, "To within eleven miles of Philadelphia. The night was very stormy."[178]

Some were passing through from wartime posts in the north. On December 25, 1781, William Hutchinson of New London Township, Chester County, who had served with the 2nd Delaware Regiment and Chester County Militia, wrote:

> *We lay at Dobbs Ferry all the fall season and until Christmas doing nothing but camp duty. The next morning, we were then ordered to Morristown and from thence to Princeton, thence to Trenton, and from thence we were transported by water to Philadelphia, thence by water to Wilmington, Delaware. At Wilmington we lay about three weeks. About this time news of the cessation of hostilities was spoken of and probably proclaimed, and also we heard of a part of the army having been disbanded, and our regiment were dismissed upon parole or furlough with orders for every man to hold himself in readiness to march at a minute's warning. And about this time we heard of the enemy having vacated New York. After this we were never called upon and received no discharge.*[179]

The Delaware Continental Regiment was still in South Carolina on January 1, 1782. Captain Robert Kirkwood visited the army headquarters at the High Hills of the Santee, a long, narrow, hilly region in the western part of Sumter County, South Carolina, "and got Liberty to retire to the Delaware State on furlough." Many days and weeks of marching followed. On March 16, the men reached Petersburgh, Virginia, where their adventures had begun. Kirkwood told us about how some of the men came home from the southern campaign: "Lts. Campbell, Anderson and Platt with myself went on to Board a vessel at the Broad Way, bound to the Head of Elk." He noted that on April 7, 1782, he "[t]ook a passage on board the Pacquett Commanded by Capt. Simpson & arrived at Newark about 8 Oclock in the evening. Total of Marches from the 13th of April 1780 untill the 7th of April 1782 was 4982 miles; omitted one night's march to the old regulating ground 24 = 5,006 miles."[180]

The convoy carrying the Delaware troops anchored at Cape May. By nightfall, April 7, 1782, the Delaware Bay was full of action. When British vessels were seen approaching, naval lieutenant Joshua Barney ordered the merchantmen to flee up into the Delaware Bay, while the armed sloop *Hyder Ally* remained behind to engage the British. Faking retreat, the *Hyder Ally*'s gun ports remained closed, and it did not fire. The trick worked. British captain Rodgers of the *General Monk* ordered the *Hyder* to surrender. Barney answered with a broadside of grape, canister and round shot that raked the deck of the British sloop, killing some sailors and marines, and then ordered his ship to port and unleashed another broadside. A few minutes later, the two sloops had drifted close enough together that the British and Americans could hear one another shouting commands. Barney gave his sailors quiet directions while, in a loud voice, ordering them to do something else. As he had apparently intended, the two vessels collided and became entangled in each other's rigging. The American sailors fastened the *General Monk* to their ship to prevent it from breaking loose and then fired broadside. The shots knocked out some of the British guns and sent the crew into confusion. After less than half an hour of close-quarters combat, both the *General Monk* and another British vessel, the *Charming Molly*, were captured. The Americans had won the day.[181]

Nor Turned About 'Til I Got Home, Locked Up in Mother's Chamber

New Englander Joseph Plumb Martin reminisced about some people he met on his way home as he marched through Wilmington:

> *We accordingly left Yorktown and we set our faces towards the Highlands of New York. It was now the month of November and winter approaching. We all wished to be nearer home.... We landed at what is called the Head of Elk, where we found the rest of our corps and some of the infantry, also a few French.... We encamped one night, while on our march, at Wilmington, a very handsome borough town on the Christiana Creek, in the state of Delaware. I was quartered for the night at a gentleman's house, who had before the war, been a sea captain.... In the morning we marched, some of us concluded to have a stimulator. I went to a house nearby where I was informed they sold liquors. When I entered the house, I saw a young woman in decent morning dishabille. I asked her if I could have any liquor there. She told me that her husband had just stepped out and would be in directly, and very politely desired me to be seated. I had sat but a minute or two when there came in from the back yard a great pot-bellied Negro man, rigged off in superfine broadcloth, ruffled shirt, bowshin and flat foot, and as black and shining as a junk bottle. "My dear," said the lady, "this*

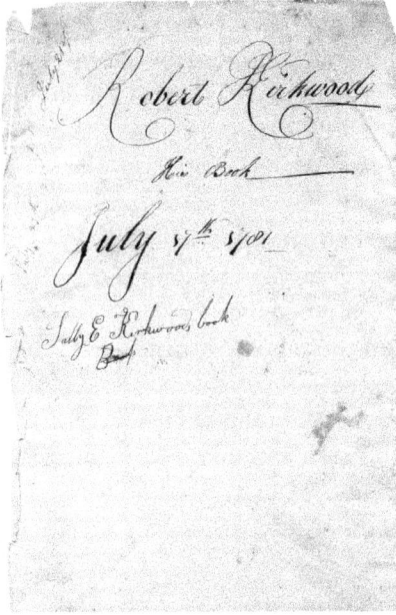

Robert Kirkwood's journal. *Delaware Historical Society.*

soldier wishes for a quart of rum." I was thunderstruck. Had not the man taken the canteen from me and measured me the liquor, I should certainly have forgotten my errand.[182]

On the final day of the year, December 31, 1782, 550 members of the French regiment of Lauzun's Legion arrived in Wilmington for the winter. The officers and men spent much of their time taking care of their horses, maintaining their equipment and engaging in guard and other military duties, as well as weapons drills and exercise. Samuel Canby, a leading Wilmington Quaker, reported that they conducted themselves "with more regularity and much more civility to the Inhabitants than any troops we have ever had in this town. Scarcely an instant of their stealing the smallest thing."[183]

MIND THE MUSIC AND THE STEP, YANKEE DOODLE DANDY

Although Cornwallis had surrendered, and many men had gone home, the war was not over. Almost one year later, in August 1782, a unit of Continental cavalry and a unit of Continental light infantry were detached by Major General Nathanael Greene to stop British and Loyalist forces from plundering plantations in the Beaufort and Colleton districts of South Carolina. Among them were Delawareans from Captain William McKennan's and Captain Paul Quenoualt's companies. They would not come home for another year.

As news of Cornwallis's defeat spread, civil unrest grew. Those who had assumed they were doing the right and proper thing by remaining loyal to Britain were growing afraid. It was inconceivable to many that British forces had gone home, and the consequences of having supported the "wrong side" were unknown. Long-term deprivations caused by the war and uncertainty about the future caused people on both sides of the political argument to lash out in rage.

People who experienced these troubled times related many horror stories. Jonathan Rumford, a wealthy grain speculator, had served as a captain in the Flying Camp Battalion of Delaware from July to December 1776, and in November 1777, he had written to Brigadier General Potter:

> *I am acquainted by Cap' Hugh Montgomery who is Just come from the River Shore that hee Counted thirty-Eight Sales of Vessels Chiefly ships & that hee heard from Mr. Whitehead Jones these had Ten Solders landed & came to his House who acquainted him That there was a fleete now in the Delaware with Several Thousand Brittish Soldears on Borde. The Ships are now Passing by I therefore send you this Inteligance & am &c. Jona. Rumford.*[184]

In spite of this service, a mob of overzealous Whigs, accusing Rumford of black market operations, invaded his home, spread firebrands through the house and fractured Rumford's skull with a blacksmith's hammer. Captain Hugh Montgomery and two captains of the militia came to his rescue, saving the house from destruction. Rumford died on July 3, 1782, in Wilmington, Delaware.[185]

When the well-armed sheriff of Kent County and his posse arrived to arrest Cheney Clow, leader of the 1778 rebellion in Little Creek Hundred, Clow barricaded himself and his wife in the house and shot at them. They shot back and hacked at the door with axes and the butts of their muskets. A member of the posse was killed, and another man was wounded. When they forced the door open, the sheriff and his party discovered that Clow's wife—who, it was believed, had loaded muskets while her husband discharged them—had been shot in the chest. Clow was taken to Dover. After four years in prison, he was accused of high treason at a Court of Oyer and Terminer on December 10, 1782. Pleading not guilty, he claimed that as captain in the British army, he was entitled to be treated as a prisoner of war. He was convicted instead of the murder of posse member Moore. Although the posse member's death had originally been considered an accident, Cheney Clow was hanged in 1788. It is said locally that Cheney Clow "went bravely to his death, singing a hymn as he walked to the gallows" and that Caesar Rodney, on the day of Clow's execution, "publicly wished he were governor only that he might pardon him."[186]

A group of displaced Loyalists plundered the residence of constable Robert Appleton, carrying him away as a captive. Upon reaching Bombay Hook, these marauders were joined by six other "pirates." When Appleton refused to preach a Methodist sermon, they ordered that a black man whip him with a rope. Appleton was forced to destroy official papers and made to promise that he would never serve papers on Tories again. When Appleton served a warrant a few weeks later on a Mr. Codrick of Bombay Hook, he was beaten again.[187]

1783: Yankee Doodle Dandy, Mind the Music, Mind the Step and with the Girls Be Handy

While all of these things were taking place, soldiers continued passing through the state, all needing food and clothing and supplies.

Captain Peter Jaquett and his men arrived home from Petersburgh, Virginia, on January 17, 1783, after a march of 720 miles.[188] Jaquett's Company, Captain Robert Kirkwood's Company, Captain William

Long Hook Farm, family home of Major Peter Jaquett. *David Ames, HABS-HAER, Library of Congress.*

McKennan's Company and Captain Paul Quenoualt's Company were all mustered out of Continental service on November 3, 1783, at Christiana Bridge.[189]

On April 11, 1783, the Continental Congress issued a proclamation "Declaring the Cessation of Arms" against Great Britain. On April 15, 1783, the preliminary articles of peace were approved by Congress. Although the Treaty of Paris, officially ending the American Revolutionary War, was not signed until September 3, 1783, a peace celebration was held that spring in New Castle, Delaware. At the request of the president of the State of Delaware, John Lyon of White Clay Creek Hundred supplied forty-one gallons of Madeira wine, forty-nine gallons of port, twenty-one gallons of rum, sugar and fruit and 212 dinners in New Castle for a celebration. Lyon was not reimbursed for these expenses until 1789.[190]

He Stuck a Feather in His Hat and Called It Macaroni

Peter Jaquett had been one of the first Delawareans to enlist in the Delaware Continental Line in 1776 and served until the end of the war in 1783. Jaquett and his comrades-in-arms were astounded when they tried to vote in the fall election. Jaquett said that George Read refused to allow the soldiers to vote because their lengthy out-of-state service meant that they "had becam Aliens and that in law and justice we had not a right to Voat." Jaquett wondered if "I should again be obliged to force a right for which I had contended for more than seven years in the feald." The election judges were unsure of how to act, and the mood of the election day crowd turned angry; as night began to fall and Read grew "anxious for the personal safety of himself and friends," he at last permitted the soldiers to vote. Jaquett claimed that Read had "persecuted every man that was active in securing the independence of this country" because they had "wrestled it away from the power of his Much loved king." Jaquett had his reasons for believing this, as Read had refused to vote for independence as a delegate to Continental Congress in 1776 and, in 1783, led the state legislature in repealing the anti-Loyalist Test Act.[191]

On December 16, 1783, George Washington passed through Wilmington on his way home to Mount Vernon. A public address signed by Town Clerk Joseph Shallcross was given:

Above: Washington's farewell address. *Library of Congress.*

Below: Treaty of Paris, 1783. British political cartoon showing John Bull throwing up his arms in despair as the devil flies away with a map labeled "America." James Gillray, artist. Published in London by W. Humphrey. *Library of Congress.*

To His Excellency, George Washington, Esq., General and Commander-in-Chief of the Armies of the United States of America.

MAY IT PLEASE
YOUR EXCELLENCY

The Burgesses and Common Council of the Borough of Wilmington, in behalf of themselves and the inhabitants thereof

When we reflect on the magnitude of the object for which we contended, and the greatness of the power we had to oppose, the boldest among us have sometimes shuddered at the prospect, while your magnanimity was our invincible shield on the gloomiest occasions.

Convinced that our humble talents cannot express in language suitable to the subject, either the grateful sensations we feel in the contemplation of your great and eminent services, or the love and admiration of your many amiable virtues which fill the bosom of the friends of freedom in America and in distant nations, yet, rather than wound that delicacy which would receive with reluctance even less than our duty and inclination prompt us to mention, we will conclude with embracing this opportunity of joining the general voice of America, which hails you as "the deliverer of our country"; and we flatter ourselves you will believe that our most fervent wishes will accompany your illustrious and long meditated retirement, with the enjoyment of health, tranquility and every other felicity.[192]

CONCLUSION

As the Revolutionary War ended, the odd juxtaposition of Delaware's bucolic setting and the violence of war invoked an urge to get life back to normal and set things right. The war had caused a disorientation that left many uncertain about their previous assumptions about life. No one had escaped these twenty years of turmoil unscathed. Many people had lost relatives and friends and, with them, their sense of stability. Others were bitter about real or imagined slights or envious of the successes of a neighbor. Some soldiers arrived home wounded in both body and spirit. Homeless and displaced people were an unfortunate part of the postwar scene, and it is said that many "became robbers, thieves and drunken beggars."[193] For those lucky enough to have a home, life would remain precarious until the economy picked up and the political schisms died down.

Until the new federal government had time to stabilize, life without England remained uncertain. When the new federal constitution was completed in September 1787, it was sent to the states for approval. Delaware was the first state to take action. On December 7, 1787, at a state convention in Dover, the new constitution was unanimously ratified, making Delaware the first state to join the Union. The Founding Fathers' insistence on separation of church and state was important. Delaware's Presbyterians, Quakers and Anglicans needed time to reaccommodate themselves to their neighbors and make room for newly arriving Methodists and Catholics.

Delaware has always seemed to have had a fiercely protective "we take care of our own" mentality that kicked in after the war. There was an unspoken expectation that residents would toe the line and blend back into the social fabric of the state. Many Loyalists were forgiven and moved back home; political leaders like John Dickinson, Caesar Rodney, George Read and Thomas McKean continued to serve in office both in Delaware and in Pennsylvania.

Dickinson was buried at Wilmington Friends Meeting. Caesar Rodney lived just long enough to see freedom established. He died in 1784 and is buried at an unmarked grave on his beloved farm, Poplar Grove (today called "Byfield"). George Read died in 1798 and is buried at Immanuel Episcopal Church in New Castle. Thomas McKean served on the Board of Trustees of the University of the State of Pennsylvania (now the University of Pennsylvania), dying in 1817. Hessians and at least one member of Lauzun's Legion remained here after the war. The French regiments' physician, Joseph Phillippe Eugene Capelle, would become a respected local doctor and a founding member of the Delaware Medical Society.

Quaker Daniel Byrnes moved first to Philadelphia, where he was active in the Pennsylvania Abolitionist Society,[194] knew Benjamin Franklin and sold his Delaware property to Blaire McLenahan, a rabid Pennsylvania Patriot. Byrnes and his family then moved to New Cornwall, New York, where son William would carry on the family's milling tradition. Captain Robert Kirkwood moved out west, rejoined the military and was scalped by an Indian in 1791.[195] Mary Vining, the "belle of the American Revolution," died unmarried in 1821. Schools and patriotic societies are named for many of the Delaware Patriots. The names of the others live on in articles, books and oral history.

NOTES

Introduction

1. Geist, "Common American Soldier."
2. Schellhammer, "John Adams's Rule of Thirds."

Chapter 1

3. For a readable and reasonable explanations of these British laws, see U.S. History, "American History," http://www.ushistory.org/us.
4. Read, *Life and Correspondence*, 30.
5. Hancock, *Liberty and Independence*, 35.
6. Pickering, *Great Britain*.

Chapter 2

7. John Dickinson, 1768, http://archives.dickinson.edu/sundries/liberty-song-1768.
8. This same language was used in the *South Carolina Gazette*, October 12, 1769.
9. Mekeel, *Relation of the Quakers*, 68.
10. Delaware Public Archives, *Revolutionary War*.
11. Read, *Life and Correspondence*, 88–89.

12. Lincoln, *Wilmington, Delaware Under Four Flags*, 81.

13. Coleman, *Thomas McKean*, 114.

14. Ibid., 113–14.

15. *Essex Gazette*, September 20, 1774.

16. Scharf, *History of Delaware*, 866.

17. Coleman, *Thomas McKean*, 138.

Chapter 3

18. Thomas McKean, letter to John Adams, Philadelphia, November 15, 1813, National Archives, Founders Online, http://founders.archives. gov/documents/Adams/99-02-02-6197.

19. Coleman, *Thomas McKean*, 135.

20. Hancock, "Thomas Robinson," 1–36. See also http://archives.delaware. gov/Collections/revolutionary%20war%20record/revguiderev. shtml#P87_1246.

21. Coleman, *Thomas McKean*, 135.

22. Christiana Historical Society, newspaper records relating to Christiana. See also http://www.museumsusa.org/museums/info/5812.

23. Journals of Congress, Resolution for a Fast, June 12, 1775.

24. Riordan, *Many Identities, One Nation*, 58–59.

25. Riordan, "Identity and Revolution."

26. Daniel Byrnes, Quaker Broadsides, 1775, Wilmington, Delaware, Haverford College Special Collections, BX7730.B994 S5 1775a.

27. Schlesinger, *Colonial Merchant and the American Revolution*, 557.

Chapter 4

28. Coleman, *Thomas McKean*, 137.

29. Letters of delegates to Congress, 1774–89, vol. 2, September 1775–December 1775.

30. Ibid.

31. McGrath, *Give Me a Fast Ship*, 38–39. See also the Fisher papers at HSD.

32. Sellers, *Genealogy of the Jaquett Family*.

33. For more on Tilton and McDonough, see Duncan, *Founders of the Medical Society of Delaware*.

34. Samuel Lockwood in Dann, *Revolution Remembered*, 166–67.

35. Captain John Barry (1745–1808) was given command of USS *Lexington*, fourteen guns, on December 7, 1775. It was the first naval commission issued by the Continental Congress.

36. Ryden, *Letters to and from Caesar Rodney*, letter no. 52.

37. Jackson, *Pennsylvania Navy*, 70.

38. Scharf, *History of Delaware*, 1:227.

39. Clark and Morgan, *Naval Documents of the American Revolution*, 5:15–16.

40. Jackson, *Pennsylvania Navy*, 51.

41. Andrew Snape-Hamond, Clark and Morgan, *Naval Documents*, 5:15–16.

42. British Archives, Public Record Office, Admiralty Records, Brit. Adm. Rec., A.D. 487, November 28, 1776.

43. *Proceedings of the Assembly of the Lower Counties on Delaware*, vol. 1.

Chapter 5

44. Laprad, "Thinking Locally, Acquiring Globally."

45. Hancock, "Revolutionary War Diary of William Adair," 154–70.

Chapter 6

46. Ryden, *Letters to and from Caesar Rodney*, letter no. 87.

47. John Haslet to Caesar Rodney, letter, dated July 6, 1776, Rodney Collection, Box 6, Folder 9, Delaware Historical Society.

48. Hancock, *Liberty and Independence*, 56.

49. Weintraub, *Iron Tears*, 71.

50. Christopher Mlynarczyk, 1st Delaware Regiment, http://1stdelawareregiment.org.

51. Ward, *Delaware Continentals*, 42. See also Gallagher, *Battle of Brooklyn*.

52. See also Kashatus, *Conflict of Conviction*.

53. Council of State of Delaware Minutes, January 1777.

54. Wilmington Friends Meeting Records. Around December 30, 1777, Jacob Bennett was captured by the British and taken aboard the ship *Pearl*. He was later released and told the Delaware House of Assembly that local residents had supplied cattle to the British during his captivity.

55. William Watts Hart Davis, "History of Bucks County," Pennsylvania Archives, 5th series, vol. 5.

56. Ward, *Delaware Continentals*, 488.

57. Samuel Patterson to George Read, letter, September 19, 1776, R.S. Rodney Collections, DHS. See also National Archives, Founders Online. Many of Patterson's men joined the Delaware Continental Regiment when the terms of enlistment for the Flying Camp expired in early December. Patterson served in the Delaware General Assembly in 1778 and as state treasurer from 1779 to 1785, http://founders.archives.gov/documents/Washington/03-08-02-0019.

Chapter 7

58. Clark and Schulz, *Delaware in the American Revolution*, 7–8, 11.

59. State of Delaware's Constitution predates the U.S. Constitution.

60. Hancock, *Liberty and Independence*, 59.

61. On November 1, Dr. William Shippen sent the Board of War "a Return of the Sick in the Hospitals of Flying Camp and Jersey Militia," in which he wrote, "The Number of sick & wounded in my department is 338–4 fifths of them are in a fair way of recovery & will soon join their respective companys. I have not yet taken charge of near 2000 that are scatter'd up & down the Country in colonial barns." National Archives, Founders Online, http://founders.archives.gov/?q=Flying%20Camp.

62. Delaware Archives, Military—Revolutionary War records, vol. 1.

63. Read, *Life and Correspondence*, 217.

64. George Read to Gertrude Read, letter, December 6, 1776, R.S. Rodney Collection, DHS.

65. Rodney, *Diary of Captain Thomas Rodney*, 12.

66. Ibid., 12–24.

67. Delaware General Assembly, *Minutes of the Council of the Delaware State*, January 1777.

68. Ibid., February 1777.

69. Samuel Lockwood in Dann, *Revolution Remembered*, 165–69.

70. Hancock, "Revolutionary War Diary of William Adair."

71. Robert Francis Seybolt, "Contemporary British Account of Sir General Howe's Military Operations in 1777," 74, American Antiquarian Society, April 1930, http://www.americanantiquarian.org/proceedings/44806860.pdf.

72. Wilmington Friends Meeting Records.

Chapter 8

73. William Hutchinson in Dann, *Revolution Remembered*, 147.

74. Founders Online, "From George Washington to Landon Carter, 27 October 1777," National Archives http://founders.archives.gov/documents/Washington/03-12-02-0018.

75. General Orders, August 26, 1777, in Chase and Lengel, *Papers of George Washington*, 11:71–72.

76. Downman, *Services of Lieut-Colonel Francis Downman*, 30.

77. Ewald, *Diary of the American War*, 76.

78. Wilmington Friends Meeting Records.

79. *Pennsylvania Evening Post*, September 6, 1777. Front-page report from the Continental Congress, August 28, 1777.

80. James McMichael, in Chase and Lengel, *Papers of George Washington*, 11:74, footnote 1, citing James McMichael's diary.

81. George Washington to John Hancock, August 29, 1777, Chase and Lengel, *Papers of George Washington*, 11:89.

82. Martin, *Philadelphia Campaign*, 41.

83. Ewald, *Diary of the American War, Honors Projects*, 77.

84. George Washington to Caesar Rodney, Wilmington, Delaware, August 31, 1777, Chase and Lengel, *Papers of George Washington*, 11:102–3.

85. Daniel Byrnes, 1842, Delaware Historical Society.

86. Burgoyne, *Enemy Views*, 171.

87. Footnote to letter from George Washington to John Hancock, September 1, 1777, Wilmington, National Archives, Founders Online, http://founders.archives.gov/documents/Washington/03-11-02-0107.

88. Ewald, *Diary of the American War*, September 8, 1777.

89. Chase and Lengel, *Papers of George Washington*, 11:110.

90. Ibid., 11:112.

91. Kirkwood, *Journal and Order Book*, 155.

92. Lieutenant (later Captain) Heinrich Carl Philipp von Feilitsch (1752–1827) of the Ansbach-Bayreuth jager company, translated by Burgoyne in *Diaries of Two Ansbach Jägers*.

93. "Journal of the Proceedings," 76.

94. Chase and Lengel, *Papers of George Washington*, 11:135.

95. Dansey, *Captured Rebel Flag*, 117.

96. Kim Burdick, A Quaker Struggles with the War. Journal of American Revolution. May 26, 2015. http://allieutenanthingsliberty.com/author/kim-burdick.

97. Chase and Lengel, *Papers of George Washington*, 11:157–58.

98. Biddle was disowned from his Quaker Meeting as early as 1775. He raised a company of soldiers composed mostly of other "fighting Quakers" and later served as quartermaster general.

99. Byrnes, *George Washington Papers*, volume 12, January–May 1793, 14–18.

100. Von Muenchhausen, *At General Howe's Side*.

101. Montresor, "Montresor Journals," September 8, 1777.

102. McGuire quoting Parker Family Papers, journal entry for September 8, 1777.

103. Burgoyne, *Enemy Views*, 173.

104. Ewald, *Diary of the American War*, September 8, 1777.

105. Captain Joseph Clark, 2nd Jersey, "Diary of Joseph Clark," 93–116.

106. Chase sent a second letter the next day enclosing Washington's September 9 letter to John Hancock, Etting, Signer Collection, Historical Society of Pennsylvania.

107. George Washington to John Hancock, September 9, 1777, Chase and Lengel, *Papers of George Washington*, 11:175.

108. Kirkwood, *Journal and Order Book*, 167.

109. George Washington to John Hancock, September 11, 1777, Chase and Lengel, *Papers of George Washington*, 11:200.

110. *American Watchman*, "Revolutionary Reminiscences," July 8, 1825.

111. Hancock, *Liberty and Independence*, 92.

112. Montresor, "Montresor Journals," 451; see also Baurmeister, *Revolution in America*, 112.

113. Von Muenchhausen, *At General Howe's Side*, 32; see also Howe to Germain, October 10, 1777, in Davies, *Documents of the American Revolution*, 14:202–9.

114. Mordecai Gist, September 14, 1777, Chase and Lengel, *Papers of George Washington*, 11:236.

115. "Journal of the Proceedings," 80.

116. McGuire, *Philadelphia Campaign*, 278, quoting Regiment von Alt Lossberg Journal (combined Battalion), letter M, fiche no. 65, M. 79–80, Lidgerwood Collection.

117. Friedrich von Wangenheim, see 1777 map, Library of Congress, https://www.loc.gov/resource/g3834w.ar135100.

118. "Revolutionary Reminiscences" from July 8 and July 22, 1825 *American Watchman* are reprinted in Hancock, *Liberty and Independence*, 107–22.

119. *American Watchman*, "Revolutionary Reminiscences," July 8, 1825.

120. Ibid.

121. Coleman, *Thomas McKean*, 216.

122. Wilmington Friends Meeting Records.

123. Ryden, *Letters to and from Caesar Rodney*, letter no. 220.

124. See Ryden, *Letters to and from Caesar Rodney*.

125. McKean to Washington, Newark, Delaware, October 8, 1777, Chase and Lengel, *Papers of George Washington*, 11:442.

126. Ward, *Delaware Continentals*, 522, citing Ambrose Serle, *American Journal*, Huntington Library, 1940.

127. Scott, *Gentleman*, 168, quoting Read, *Life and Correspondence*, 276.

128. *American Watchman*, "Revolutionary Reminiscences," July 8, 1825.

129. Independence Seaport Museum, "Man O War Blown to Bits," http://www.phillyseaport.org/ManOWar.

130. *American Watchman*, "Revolutionary Reminiscences," July 22, 1825. For more on Dr. Nicholas Way, see Duncan, *Founders of the Medical Society of Delaware*, 75.

Chapter 9

131. Bodle, *Valley Forge Winter*, 176, quoting N. Greene's letter to George Washington, February 15, 1778, George Washington Papers, Library of Congress.

132. Wayne to Washington, February 25, 1778, George Washington Papers, Library of Congress.

133. John Barry to George Washington, March 9, 1778, National Archives, Founders Online, http://founders.archives.gov/documents/Washington/03-14-02-0080.

134. Smallwood to Washington, March 9–10, 1778, National Archives, Founders Online, http://founders.archives.gov/documents/Washington/03-14-02-0089.

135. Ryden, *Letters to and from Caesar Rodney*.

Chapter 10

136. Scott, Gentleman, 172.

137. Rodney to McKean, Dover, March 9, 1778, McKean Papers, Historical Society of Pennsylvania.

138. Hancock, *Liberty and Independence*, 134.

139. Caesar Rodney to Henry Laurence, Dover, April 24, 1778, no. 1452, http://archives.delaware.gov/eBooks/DelawareArchives/DPA-

MilitaryRecords-Vol3.pdf. Clowe's land was near the Delaware-Maryland line, near Gravelly Branch Bridge.

140. Howard, Manuscripts of Earl of Carlisle.

141. See Thomas Gilpin, Exiles in Virginia…, 1778–1848, http://quod. lib.umich.edu/c/clementsmss/umich-wcl-M-4153gil?view=text.

142. Ward, *Delaware Continentals*, 261.

143. Riordan, *Many Identities, One Nation*, 66.

144. Van Doren, *Secret History of the American Revolution*, 96.

145. Lengel, *General George Washington*, 292.

146. Ryden, *Letters to and from Caesar Rodney*, letter no. 273.

147. Delaware General Assembly, Minutes of the Council of the Delaware State, 1776–92.

148. For related illustrations, please see Zlatich and Windrow, General Washington's Army.

149. Primary Documents of American History, http://loc.gov/rr/program/ bib/ourdocs/articles.html.

Chapter 11

150. Kim Burdick, "Lafayette's Second Voyage to America: Lafayette and l'Hermione," *Journal of the American Revolution*, April 20, 2015. http:// allieutenanthingsliberty.com/author/kim-burdick.

151. Delaware Archives 111, 1271 and Minutes, 340, 342, in *Revolutionary War in Three Volumes: Volume Three and Index*.

152. *American Watchman*, "Revolutionary Reminiscences," July 8, 1825.

153. Ward, *Delaware Continentals*, 288–314.

154. Patterson to Washington, May 30, 1779, National Archives, Founders Online, http://founders.archives.gov/documents/ Washington/03-20-02-0641.

155. Ryden, *Letters to and from Caesar Rodney*, 413.

156. Ward, *Delaware Continentals*, 316.

157. Ryden, *Letters to and from Caesar Rodney*. See also Ward, *Delaware Continentals*, 316. Major John Patten (April 26, 1746–December 26, 1800) was from Kent County, Delaware. Taken prisoner in Battle of Camden, South Carolina, he was paroled in 1781 and is said to have walked home alone from Charleston, South Carolina.

158. Ward, *Delaware Continentals*, 312–19.

159. William Hutchinson in Dann, *Revolution Remembered*, 154.

160. Kirkwood, *Journal and Order Book*, 10.
161. Kim Burdick, "An Overview of Robert Kirkwood in the Southern Campaign of the American Revolution," Academia, https://www.academia.edu/15176371.
162. Clark and McAllister, *Delaware in the American Revolution*, 23. See also Ward, Delaware Continentals, and related websites http://1stdelawareregiment.org and www.halebyrnes.org.

Chapter 12

163. Van Buskirk, *Generous Enemies*, 42.
164. Raphael, *People's History*, 172.
165. Delaware Archives, *Revolutionary War in Three Volumes*, Sussex County, 1,302–4, https://play.google.com/store/books/details?id=MwojAQAAI AAJ&rdid=book-MwojAQAAIAAJ&rdot=1.
166. Kim Burdick, "A Quaker Struggles with the War," *Journal of the American Revolution* (May 26, 2015), https://allthingsliberty.com/2015/05/a-quaker-struggles-with-the-war.
167. Delaware Archives, *Revolutionary War in Three Volumes*, 3:1,357–58.
168. Hancock, *Liberty and Independence*, 88.

Chapter 13

169. Please see http://xenophongroup.com/mcjoynt/ep_web.htm and http://www.w3r-us.org/history/library/seligreptde4.pdf.
170. Benjamin, *Genealogy of the Family*, September 5, 1777.
171. Tallmadge, *Journal*, 759.
172. Reeves, *Pennsylvania Magazine of History and Biography*, 235–56.
173. Martin, *Private Yankee Doodle Dandy*, 192.
174. Tallmadge, *Journal*, 759–60.
175. Kirkwood, *Journal and Order Book*, October 27, 1781.

Chapter 14

176. Delaware General Assembly, *Minutes of the Council of the Delaware State*, October 27, 1781, 159.

177. John Dickinson, Delaware General Assembly, *Minutes of the Council of the Delaware State*, November 13, 1781, 166.

178. Benjamin, *Genealogy of the Family*, 24–38.

179. Hutchinson in Dann, *Revolution Remembered*, 155.

180. Kirkwood, *Journal and Order Book*, 30.

181. Understanding the American Revolution and Beyond, "Captain Joshua Barney Wins the Battle of Delaware Bay," http://www.revolutionary-war-and-beyond.com/joshua-barney-wins-battle-of-delaware-bay.html.

182. Martin, *Private Yankee Doodle Dandy*, 211.

183. Selig, *W3R in the State of Delaware*, http://www.w3r-us.org/history/library/seligreptde4.pdf.

184. See also RootsWeb, http://freepages.genealogy.rootsweb.ancestry.com/~jemjr/2145.htm.

185. Hancock, *Liberty and Independence*, 102.

186. Read, *Life and Correspondence*, 324. See also http://davidclowartist.tripod.com/clow/index.html.

187. Calhoon and Barnes, *Tory Insurgents*.

188. Jaquett, "Pension Application of Peter Jaquett."

189. U.S. Army Center of Military History, 198th Signal Battalion.

190. Delaware Archives, *Revolutionary War in Three Volumes*, 3:1,483.

191. Riordan, *Many Identities, One Nation*, 85–86, quoting letter from Jaquett to Caesar Rodney dated November 4, 1804, and reprinted in Hancock, "Loaves and Fishes," 150–58, quote 151.

192. Montgomery, "Reminiscences of Wilmington," 58–59. Elizabeth Montgomery believed that this speech was probably written by Jacob Broom.

Conclusion

193. Scharf, *History of Delaware*.

194. By 1860, slavery was extinct in Wilmington and disappearing in lower New Castle County. Even in Sussex County, the ratio of free to slave was one to three, but the General Assembly hesitated to take the final step. Abolitionists almost succeeded in 1847, but one vote kept them from success.

195. Find-a-Grave, "Captain Robert Kirkwood," http://www.findagrave.com/cgi-bin/fg.cgi?page=gr&GRid=71818366.

SELECTED BIBLIOGRAPHY

Archives

Researchers interested in studying life in Delaware in the American Revolution should begin their research at these institutions.

Delaware Historical Society. 505 North Market Street, Wilmington, DE, 19801. Phone: (302) 655-7161. http://www.dehistory.org.

Delaware Public Archives. 121 Martin Luther King Jr. Boulevard, North Dover, DE, 19901. Phone: (302) 744-5000. http://archives.delaware.gov/collections/revolutionary_war_record/revguiderev.shtml.

Friends Historical Library, McCabe Library, Swarthmore College. Swarthmore, PA, 19081. Phone: (610) 328-8496. http://www.swarthmore.edu/friends-historical-library.

University of Delaware. Special Collections, Morris Library. 181 South College Avenue, Newark, DE, 19717. Phone: (302) 831-6089. https://library.udel.edu/spec/?s=&pr=specials&cq=&query=Washington+Rochambeau.

Primary Documents

Anderson, Enoch. "Personal Recollections of Captain Enoch Anderson, an Officer of the Delaware Regiments in the Revolutionary War." Edited by Henry Hobart. *Historical and Biographical Papers of the Historical Society of Delaware* 2, no. 16 (1896).

André, John. *Major André's Journal: Operations of the British Under Lieutenant Generals Sir William Howe and Sir Henry Clinton, June 1777 to November, 1778.* Tarrytown, NY: William Abbott, 1930.

Baurmeister, Adjutant General Major. *Revolution in America: Confidential Letters and Journals 1776–1784 of Adjutant General Major Baurmeister of the Hessian Forces.* Translated and annotated by Bernhard A. Uhlendorf. New Brunswick, NJ: Rutgers University Press, 1957.

Benjamin, Samuel. "Extracts from Lieutenant Benjamin's Revolutionary Diary." In *Genealogy of the Family of Lieut. Samuel Benjamin and Tabitha Livermore, His Wife, Compiled by Mary L. Benjamin.* Winthrop, ME, 1900.

Burgoyne, Bruce, trans. and ed. *Diaries of Two Ansbach Jägers.* Westminster, MD, 2007.

———. *Enemy Views: The American Revolution as Recorded by Hessian Participants.* Bowie, MD: Heritage Books Inc., 1996.

Chase, Philander, and Edward G. Lengel, eds. *The Papers of George Washington.* Revolutionary War Series, vol. 11. Charlottesville: University of Virginia, 2001.

Chase, Philander, and Frank E. Grizzard Jr., eds. *The Papers of George Washington.* Revolutionary War Series, vol. 6. Charlottesville: University of Virginia, 1994.

Clark, William Bell, and William James Morgan. *Naval Documents of the American Revolution.* Washington, D.C.: Naval Historical Center, n.d.

Continental Congress. Letters of delegates to Congress, 1774–89. Vol. 2, September 1775–December 1775. American Memory, Library of Congress.

Dann, John C., ed. *The Revolution Remembered: Eyewitness Accounts of the War for Independence.* Chicago: University of Chicago Press, 1980.

Dansey, William. *Captured Rebel Flag: The Letters of Captain William Dansey, 33rd Regiment of Foot, 1776–1777.* Ken Trottman, 2010. Huntingdon, UK: Ken Trotman Publishing.

Davies, K.G., ed. *Documents of the American Revolution, 1770–1783.* Colonial Office Series. 21 vols. Shannon, IE: Irish University Press, 1972–81.

Delaware Archives. RG 1800.099. A series of thirteen manuscript boxes, one volume of original records and three published volumes. http://archives.delaware.gov/collections/revolutionary_war_record/revguiderev.shtml.

Delaware Archives. Military—Revolutionary War records, transcribed and indexed by the Delaware Public Archives. Vol. 1. Wilmington, DE: Mercantile Printing, 1911.

Delaware General Assembly. *Minutes of the Council of the Delaware State,* 1776–92. N.p.: General Books LLC reprint. See also https://archive.org/stream/minutescouncild00assegoog/minutescouncild00assegoog_djvu.txt.

Delaware Historical Society. http://librarycompany.org/Economics/PEAESGuide/dhs.htm. Including the *Delaware History Journal,* published semiannually by the society; the Brown Collection of Rodney Letters and Papers; the Rodney Collection of Letters and Journal; and the William Dansey letters.

Delaware Public Archives Commission, Delaware Archives. *Revolutionary War in Three Volumes*. Wilmington, DE: Charles L. Story Publisher, 1919.

Ewald, Johann. *Diary of the American War: A Hessian Journal*. Edited by Joseph P. Tustin. Princeton, NJ, 1976.

Gallagher, John. *Battle of Brooklyn, 1776*. New York: Sarpedon Publishers, 1995.

Grizzard, Frank E., ed. *The Papers of George Washington*. Revolutionary War Series, vol. 10. Charlottesville: University of Virginia, 2000.

Howard, George James, Earl of Carlisle. Manuscripts of Earl of Carlisle, printed for HMSO. London: Eyre and Spottiswood, 1897.

Howe, William. *British Army Orders, 1775–1778*. N.p., n.d. https://archive. org/stream/collectionsvolu03socigoog#page/n514/mode/2up.

Jaquett, Peter. "Pension Application of Peter Jaquett S46500 DE." Southern Campaign, American Revolution Pension Statements & Rosters. Transcribed and annotated by C. Leon Harris. Revised June 24, 2013. http://revwarapps.org/s46500.pdf.

"Journal of the Proceedings of the Army Under the Command of Sir Wm Howe in the Year 1777." In *A Contemporary British Account of General Sir William Howe's Military Operations in 1777*. Edited by Robert Francis Seybolt. N.p.: American Antiquarian Society, 1930.

Kirkwood, Robert. *The Journal and Order Book of Captain Robert Kirkwood of the Delaware Regiment of the Continental Line*. Edited by Joseph Brown Turner. Philadelphia: Historical Society of Pennsylvania, 1910. Nabu Public Domain Reprint.

Martin, Joseph Plumb. *Private Yankee Doodle Dandy, Being a Narrative of Some of the Adventures of a Revolutionary Soldier*. Edited by George E. Scheer. N.p.: Eastern National, 1962.

McKean, Thomas. Collection 405, Thomas McKean Papers. Historical Society of Pennsylvania, 1300 Locust Street, Philadelphia, PA, 19107. http://www.hsp.org. Creator: McKean, Thomas, 1734–1817, 1757–1892 (bulk 1757–1815), thirteen boxes, 2.6 linear feet.

Mekeel, Arthur J. *The Relation of the Quakers to the American Revolution*. Lanham, MD: University Press of America, 1979

Montgomery, Elizabeth. "Reminiscences of Wilmington, 1851." Historical Society of Delaware, n.d.

Montgomery, Joseph. *A Sermon Produced at Christiana Bride and New Castle*. Philadelphia: Humphries, 1775.

Montresor, John. "The Montresor Journals." Edited by G.D. Delaplaine. Collections of the New York Historical Society, 1881 (1882).

National Archives and Records Administration, Washington, D.C., Founders Online. National Historical Publications and Records Commission. http://founders.archives.gov/documents/Washington. Including the Papers of the Continental Congress (available online) and Revolutionary War Pension and Bounty-Land Warrant Application Files (M804) [RWPF] (available online).

Peebles, John. *John Peebles' American War: The Diary of a Scottish Grenadier, 1776–1782*. Edited by Ira D. Gruber. Mechanicsburg, PA: Stackpole Books, 1998.

Proceedings of the Assembly of the Lower Counties on Delaware, 1770–1776, of the Constitutional Convention of 1776, and of the House of Assembly of the Delaware State, 1776–1781. Newark: University of Delaware Press, 1986.

Read, William T. *Life and Correspondence of George Read*. Philadelphia: JB Lippincott and Company, 1870.

Revolutionary War in Three Volumes: Volume Three and Index. Public Archives Commission of Delaware. Available at Cornell University Library. Wilmington, DE: Chas. L. Story Company Press. https://archive.org/stream/cu31924092229107/cu31924092229107_djvu.txt.

Rodney, Thomas. *Diary of Captain Thomas Rodney, 1776–1777*. Historical Society of Delaware, 1888. An on-demand reprint by Kessinger Publication.

The Royal Commission on the Losses and Services of the American Loyalists, 1783 to 1785…. Oxford, UK: Roxburghe Club, 1915. Includes notes of Daniel Parker Coke, a commissioner. Included among these Loyalists are Dr. John Watson of New Castle and Thomas Robinson of Sussex County.

Ryden, George H. *Letters to and from Caesar Rodney, 1756–1784*. Philadelphia: Historical Society of Delaware, 1933.

Tallmadge, Samuel. *Orderly Books of the Fourth New York Regiment, 1778–1780, the Second New York Regiment, 1780–1783; Journal of Samuel Tallmadge*. Albany: University of the State of New York, 1932.

Tilton, James. *Timoleon's Biographical History of Dionysius, Tyrant of Delaware*. Edited by John Munroe. Newark: University of Delaware Press, 1958.

U.S. Army Center of Military History. 198th Signal Battalion. Lineage and Honors Information. http://www.history.army.mil/html/forcestruc/lineages/branches/sc/0198scbn.htm.

Von Muenchhausen, Friedrich. *At General Howe's Side: 1776–1778: The Diary of Admiral Howe's Aide de Camp*. Translated by Ernst Kipping and edited by Samuel Steele Smith. Monmouth, NJ: Philip Freneau Press, 1974.

Wilmington Friends Meeting. *Misc. Reports of the Committees, 1732–1835.* Friends Historical Library, Swarthmore College, Swarthmore, Pennsylvania.

Secondary

Amott, David, Eric Gollannek and David Ames. *A History of Delaware Roads and a Guide to Researching Them.* Center for Historic Architecture and Design, University of Delaware, May 2006.

Becker, Carl. *The Eve of the Revolution.* Ithaca, NY, 1918.

Bodle, Wayne. *The Valley Forge Winter: Civilians and Soldiers in War.* University Park: Pennsylvania State University Press, 2002.

Byrnes, Daniel. *George Washington Papers.* Edited by Christine S. Patrick and John C. Pinheiro. Presidential Series. Vol. 12, January–May 1793. Charlottesville: University Press of Virginia, 2005.

Calhoon, Robert M., and Timothy M. Barnes. *Tory Insurgents: The Loyalist Perception.* Columbia: University of South Carolina Press, 2010.

Clark, Ellen McAllister, and Emily Schulz. *Delaware in the American Revolution.* Anderson House. Exhibition catalogue, Society of Cincinnati. Washington, D.C, 2002.

Coleman, John. *Thomas McKean: Forgotten Leader of the Revolution.* Rockaway, NJ: American Faculty Press, 1975.

Downman, Francis. *Services of Lieut-Colonel Francis Downman, R.A. Between the Years 1758 and 1784.* Edited by F.A. Whinyates. Woolwich: Royal Artillery Institution, 1898.

Duncan, William H. *Founders of the Medical Society of Delaware.* Wilmington, DE: Cedar Tree Press, 2007.

Edson, Edith McLane. "A James Peale Puzzle: Captain Allen McLane's Encounter with British Dragoons." *Pennsylvania Magazine of History and Biography* 125, no. 4 (October 2001): 375–92.

Ewald, Johann. "Diary of the American War." In *Honors Projects*, Paper 20 (2001). http://digitalcommons.iwu.edu/history_honproj/20.

Geist, Christopher. "A Common American Soldier." *Colonial Williamsburg Journal* (Autumn 2004). https://www.history.org/Foundation/journal/Autumn04/soldier.cfm.

Gibson, George, ed. *The Collected Essays of Richard S. Rodney on Early Delaware.* Society of Colonial Wars in the State of Delaware. Wilmington, DE, 1975.

Hancock, Harold B. *The Delaware Loyalists*. Wilmington: Historical Society of Delaware, 1940. Available as a Google e-book.

———. *Liberty and Independence: Delaware During the American Revolution*. Wilmington: Delaware American Revolution Bicentennial Commission, 1976.

———. "Loaves and Fishes." *Delaware History* 14 (1970): 150–58.

———. "New Castle County Loyalists." *Delaware History* 4 (September 1951): 315–53.

———. "The Revolutionary War Diary of William Adair." *Delaware History* 13 (1968–69): 154–70.

———. "Robinson, Loyalist Chief." *Sunday Morning Star*, September 1940.

———. "Thomas Robinson: Delaware's Most Prominent Loyalist." *Delaware Historical Society* 10, no. 1 (March 1950): 1–36. Wilmington, Delaware.

Jackson, John W. *The Pennsylvania Navy, 1775–1781: Defense of the Delaware*. New Brunswick, NJ: Rutgers University Press, 1974.

Kashatus, William. *Conflict of Conviction*. Lanham, MD: University Press of America, 1990.

Laprad, Kathryn. "Thinking Locally, Acquiring Globally: The Loockerman Family of Delaware, 1630–1790." Master's thesis, Newark University of Delaware, 2010. http://udspace.udel.edu/handle/19716/5742.

Lengel, Edward G. *General George Washington: A Military Life*. New York: Random House, 2005.

Lincoln, Anna T. *Wilmington, Delaware Under Four Flags*. Rutland, VT: Tuttle Publishing Company, 1937.

Marietta, Jack D. *The Reformation of American Quakerism, 1748–1783*. Philadelphia: University of Pennsylvania Press, 1984.

Martin, David G. *The Philadelphia Campaign, June 1777–July 1778*. Conshohocken, PA: Combined Books Inc., 1993.

Mary Vining Chapter DAR. http://www.darmaryvining.org/about.htm.

McGrath, Tim. *Give Me a Fast Ship: The Continental Navy and America's Revolution at Sea*. New York: NAL Caliber Penguin Random House, 2014.

McGuire, Thomas J. *The Philadelphia Campaign: Brandywine and the Fall of Philadelphia*. Mechanicsburg, PA: Stackpole Books, 2006.

Montgomery, Elizabeth. *Reminiscences of Wilmington in Familiar Village Tales, Ancient and New*. Wilmington, DE, 1851.

Munroe, John. *Colonial Delaware: A History*. Millwood, NY: KTO Press, 1978.

———. *Federalist Delaware, 1775–1815*. New Brunswick, NJ: Rutgers University Press, 1954.

Pickering, Dan. *Great Britain: The Statutes at Large….* Cambridge: Benthem, for C. Bathhurst; 1762–1869.

Pickett, Russ. Delaware Military History. www.militaryheritage.org.

Raphael, Ray. *A People's History of the American Revolution: How Common People Shaped the Fight for Independence* Reprint ed. New York: Harper Perennial, 2002.

Reed, John F. *Campaign to Valley Forge: July 1–December 19, 1777.* Philadelphia: Pioneer Press, 1963.

Reeves, Enos. *Pennsylvania Magazine of History and Biography* 21, no. 2 (1897): 235–56. Published by Historical Society of Pennsylvania. http://www.jstor.org/stable/20085744 09/6-7.

Rice, Howard C., and Anne S.K. Brow. *American Campaigns of Rochambeau's Army, 1780, 1781, 1782, 1783.* 2 vols. Princeton, NJ, 1972.

Riordan, Liam. "Identity and Revolution: Everyday Life and Crisis in Three Delaware River Towns." Pennsylvania History. https://ojs.libraries.psu.edu/index.php/phj/article/download/25350/25119.

———. *Many Identities, One Nation: The Revolution and Its Legacy in the Mid-Atlantic.* Philadelphia: University of Pennsylvania Press, 2007.

Rowe, G.S. *Thomas McKean: The Shaping of an American Republicanism.* Boulder: University of Colorado Press, 1978.

Scharf, J. Thomas. *History of Delaware, 1609–1888.* 2 vols. Philadelphia: I.J. Richards and Company, 1888.

Schellhammer, Michael. "John Adams's Rule of Thirds." *Journal of American Revolution* (February 11, 2013).

Schlesinger, Arthur M. *Colonial Merchant and the American Revolution.* Athenaeum, NY, 1968.

Scott, Jane Harrington. *A Gentleman as Well as a Whig: Caesar Rodney and the American Revolution.* National Society of the Colonial Dames of America in the State of Delaware. Newark: University of Delaware Press, 2000.

Selig, Robert A. *W3R in the State of Delaware.* 2003. State of Delaware and Delaware State Sons of the American Revolution. http://w3r-us.org/history/library/learnmor.htm and http://history.delaware.gov/preservation/research/topics.shtml.

Sellers, Edwin Jaquett. Genealogy of the Jaquett Family. https://archive.org/stream/genealogyofjaque00sell_0/genealogyofjaque00sell_0_djvu.txt.

Van Buskirk, Judith L. *Generous Enemies: Patriots and Loyalists in Revolutionary New York.* Early American Studies. Philadelphia: University of Pennsylvania Press, n.d.

Van Doren, Carl. *Secret History of the American Revolution.* New York: Viking Press, 1941.

Ward, Christopher. *The Delaware Continentals, 1776–1783.* Wilmington: Historical Society of Delaware, 1941. Delaware Heritage Commission reprint, 2001.

Weintraub, Stanley. *Iron Tears: Rebellion in America, 1775–1783*. London: Simon & Schuster, 2005.

Werner, Emmy E. *In Pursuit of Liberty: Coming of Age in the American Revolution*. Westport, CT: Praeger Publishers, 2006.

Zlatich, Marko, and Martin Windrow. *General Washington's Army, 1775–78*. Edited by Martin Windrow and illustrated by Peter Copeland. Men-at-Arms Series, 273. N.p.: Osprey Paperback, 1994.

INDEX

ABOUT THE AUTHOR

Kim Burdick is the founder and chairman of the American Revolution Round Table of Northern Delaware. From 2003 to 2009, she served as project director of the 225th anniversary of the Yorktown Campaign (W3R), including the coordination of celebrations and lobbying efforts in nine states and Washington, D.C. In recognition of these efforts to celebrate French assistance in the American Revolution, Kim was awarded Les Palmes Académiques at Yorktown Days 2009 by Ambassador Pierre Vimont and Consul General Michel Schaffhauser. In 2008, she moved with her family to the Hale-Byrnes House in Stanton, Delaware—once the home of Delaware Quaker Daniel Byrnes. A life member of American Friends of Lafayette and president of the George Washington Society of Delaware, Burdick has been an instructor of American history at Delaware Technical and Community College since 2004. Kim has served both as chairman of the Delaware Humanities Council and as a member of the Board of Advisors of the National Trust for Historic Preservation.

www.ingramcontent.com/pod-product-compliance
Lightning Source LLC
Chambersburg PA
CBHW060800100426
42813CB00004B/897